Malachi

Messenger of
Divine Love

Malachi

Messenger of Divine Love

Thomas J. Delaughter

Insight Press, Incorporated

Published by

Insight Press, Inc.
3939 Gentilly Blvd.
New Orleans, LA   70126

Printed by

Christian Litho
Zachary, LA   70791

Library of Congress Cataloging in Publication Data

DeLaughter, Thomas J
    Malachi, messenger of divine love.

    Bibliography: p.
    1. Bible. O. T. Malachi--Commentaries. I. Title.
BS1675.3.D44   224'.99'06   75-40410
ISBN0-914520-07-5

Dedicated to

Lurlean

helpmeet and homemaker,
whose faith, prayers, encouragement, and
support have inspired me
in all of my work.

Preface

TO THE READER

Malachi: Messenger of Divine Love has been written as a result of studies in this last book of the Old Testament which have been offered in classes in Hebrew and in English exegesis at New Orleans Baptist Theological Seminary. Students who have participated in these studies have been a challenge to the writer and have given encouragement in this endeavor.

The reader will find this work to be a verse-by-verse exegesis of the text of Malachi. Scholarly works on the text have been utilized in this study as well as works on introduction, theology, history, and Bible dictionaries and encyclopedias. It is hoped that this volume will provide information and inspiration for all who are concerned about a serious study and a proclamation of this unique prophetic book.

A serious effort is made to understand the meaning of the following phrases which are found in the book of Malachi:

Jacob I have loved, but Esau I have hated; every one who does evil is good in the sight of the Lord; the Lord whom you seek will suddenly come to his temple; will a man rob God; it is vain to serve God; the book of remembrance of those who reverenced the Lord; the sun of righteousness; the sending of Elijah the prophet before the great and terrible day of the Lord comes.

Gratitude is expressed to all of my teachers and colleagues in Old Testament, especially to George W. Harrison, Dean J. Hardee Kennedy, and the late J. Wash Watts for their encouragement and help in making this work possible. Dr. John Olen Strange provided invaluable assistance in reading the manuscript and offering helpful suggestions regarding organization and interpretation. I also am indebted to the administration and trustees of New Orleans Baptist Theological Seminary for providing a sabbatical leave from my work at the seminary, enabling me to complete the studies in Malachi which have engaged my attention for a number of years. I also wish to thank Mrs. Charlotte Madison, who served as my secretary when this work was being completed, for her invaluable help in preparing the manuscript. Many people to whom I have taught the book of Malachi in Bible conferences and to whom I have preached have been kind in their remarks and generous in their expressions of encouragement. These have provided invaluable help and stimulation in this endeavor. Acknowledgment of a profound debt to a host of scholars from whom materials have been taken has been made in footnotes and bibliography.

November, 1975   *Thomas J. Delaughter*

Contents

I.	Background and Introduction	11
II.	Divine Love Declared	33
III.	Divine Love Dishonored	53
IV.	Divine Love Threatens Punishment	75
V.	Divine Love Despises Unfaithfulness	91
VI.	Divine Love Personally Manifested	105
VII.	Divine Love Demands Obedience	119
VII.	Divine Love Expressed in Righteous Judgment	131
	Selected Bibliography	149

I. Background and Introduction

A NEW DRAMA BEGINS

The curtain opens, and a new drama begins. The people of Judah who have spent seventy years in Babylonian captivity are being liberated. When Cyrus, the Persian monarch, conquered Babylon, one of his first official acts was to issue a decree allowing Hebrew captives to return to their native land (cf. Isa. 44:28; Jer. 25:12-14; 2 Chron. 36: 22-23; Ezra 1:1-4). He not only permitted them to return, but he ordered the people in all the realms where the Jews sojourned to help them with material possessions, including "the freewill offering for the house of God" which they were to build in Jerusalem (cf. Ezra 1:4). In addition, Cyrus restored the vessels of the temple which had been taken to Babylon when Nebuchadnezzar's armies sacked Jerusalem and destroyed its house of worship in 586 B.C. (cf. Ezra 1:7-11). He also gave the Jews a generous grant of money to be used in the erection of the temple (cf. Ezra 3:7).

The decree of the return of the people to their native land (ca. 538-535 B.C.) marked the beginning of the significant era which is commonly known as the post-exilic period. It extended to the close of the Old Testament time, including the inter-biblical period. Response to the decree of Cyrus appeared to be immediate and enthusiastic on the part of some of the Jewish people. The decree marked a new beginning and a new day in spite of the hardships and sufferings which were encountered in the realization of a long awaited hope. It is correctly designated as a time of restoration, reorientation, reconstruction, and renewal.

The implementation of the decree was a gradually unfolding drama to be enacted upon a new stage with different scenery and with a new set of objectives. Some old lines had to be recalled, and some new ones were to be learned. It was to be accomplished by almost none, if any, of the people who went out with the captives seventy years before (cf. Hag. 2:3). The first group to return was led by Sheshbazzar who was appointed governor or a magistrate of some sort by Cyrus (cf. Ezra 5:13-16). We cannot be absolutely certain about Sheshbazzar's name or his high political position. Although it has not been proven, Sheshbazzar has been regarded as another name for Zerubbabel (cf. Ezra 2:21). Some interpreters consider Shenazzar to be another name for Sheshbazzar (cf. 1 Chron. 3:18). He is identified as a son of Jehoiachin, the exiled king of Judah, and a prince of the Davidic line (cf. Ezra 5:19).

Almost no information regarding the accomplishments and fortunes of the first group of returnees is available to us. It is known that they brought the vessels of the temple and laid the foundations for the new temple which was to be built in Jerusalem (cf. Ezra 5:14-17). It is safe to conclude that they began some sort of worship with appropriate sacrifices and offerings.

Another group of returning captives was led by Zerubbabel, the next governor, and Joshua, the high priest (cf. Ezra 2:1-2, 64-67). Zerubbabel was a son of Shealtiel, Jehoiachin's eldest son, and was Sheshbazzar's nephew. From the accounts in Ezra it is concluded that there was a very short interval of time between the return of this group and those who were brought back by Sheshbazzar. According to Ezra, it appears that the second group arrived and joined with the first ones in laying the foundation of the house of God (cf. Ezra 3:1-11). It is possible, however, that the foundation of the temple was begun by the first group and completed by the second. It may be that the efforts of Sheshbazzar were thwarted and that which he had built was destroyed by enemy forces. If this is the case, a new beginning was made by Zerubbabel. It is known that the efforts of the latter were hindered (cf. Ezra 4:1-6). In fact, the building efforts were discontinued for a period of fifteen years (cf. Ezra 4:23-24; Hag. 1:2-3).

Regarding outside opposition, John Bright has observed:
Although Nehemiah had full authority from the King, he had powerful foes who resented his presence and wasted no chance to put obstacles in his way. Chief among these was Sanballat . . . governor of the province of Samaria . . . with him was Tobiah, governor of the province of Ammon in Transjordan . . . with these two was associated (chs. 2:19; 6:1, 6) a certain Geshem (Gashmu) "the Arab," who is known from inscriptions as a powerful chieftan of Qedar (Dedan) in northwestern Arabia. Under nominal Persian control, his rule extended westward across Sinai as far as Egypt, and included Edom, the Negeb, and southern Judah. [1]
Nehemiah arrived in Jerusalem after the temple had been built, but the enemies who opposed him were the same ones who earlier sought to thwart the efforts of the temple builders (cf. Ezra 4:1ff.). This opposition came about because the Samaritans who were established in the land opposed the Jews and sought to hinder them in their efforts to rebuild and to become established as a nation. They requested to be allowed to assist the Jews in the erection of the temple. This request was denied (cf. Ezra 4:1-3). It is not known why the new Jerusalem community did not want their nearest neighbors and kinsmen to have any part with them. It is surmised that it was because of a revival of the old Northern and Southern Kingdom political animosities and theological differences which at one time were focused in the Mosaic tradition at Shiloh and the Davidic

[1] John Bright, *A History of Israel* (2nd ed.; Philadelphia: Westminster Press, 1972), p. 383.

covenant theology at Jerusalem. Social, racial, and economic problems could have contributed to the conflict.

When their request was denied, the Samaritans then sought to discourage and intimidate the builders by making them afraid to build and frustrating their purpose (cf. Ezra 4:4-5). When these efforts failed, they charged the Jews with intentions of throwing off the yoke of their masters (cf. Ezra 4:17-24). This resulted in a decree that brought the erection of the temple to a halt. After some time the accusations of insubordination and revolt was proved to be fallacious or inconsequential, and the ban against their building was lifted.

The work was not resumed, however, until Haggai and Zechariah, two of the three great post-exilic prophets, began to preach to the leaders and to all the people regarding their failure to build God a house. They declared that the misfortunes and sufferings which has befallen them were chastisements of God because of their failure to rebuild the temple (cf. Hag. 1:7-11). The people responded to the preaching of the prophets and completed the temple in spite of opposition, discouragement, and financial difficulties (cf. Ezra 5:1-2; 6:6-18; Hag. 1:12-15; Zech. 4:6-10a). This was the first of three significant events in the reconstruction of Jerusalem. The other two were the rebuilding of the walls of Jerusalem by Nehemiah, and the renewal of the covenant by Ezra (cf. Neh. 2:17ff.; 9:38).

The foregoing facts set the stage for the beginnings of the new community. Other persons are yet to be a part of this unfolding drama. Among these is Malachi, a unique and influential post-exilic prophet. Following him, if indeed they were not his contemporaries, are Ezra and Nehemiah. They appeared with new recruits and made further efforts to stabilize the community in its political, material, and spiritual welfare.

THE AUTHORSHIP AND DATE OF MALACHI

Many scholars say that the book of Malachi was written by an unknown author. Numerous works on Old Testament introduction will bear this out.[1] The generally accepted opinion is that the book of Malachi is an anonymous writing and that the name given in 1:1 is borrowed from 3:1 where the word is a common noun to be translated "my messenger." This arrangement is considered to have been made by an editor or a compiler of The Book of the Twelve. In this usage, "my messenger" may have reference to any faithful messenger of God in the same way that "Theophilus" may be applied to any "God lover" (cf. Luke 1:3; Acts 1:1). Thus the title "my messenger" would be descriptive of the work of a prophet. Another argument given in favor of anonymity is that Malachi as a name is not found anywhere else in the Scriptures. Some scholars declare emphatically that no Hebrew parent would name his son Malachi.

The title verse (1:1) in the Septuagint reads, "the oracle of the word of the Lord to Israel by the hand of his angel." This translation has been taken by some in support of a tradition that Malachi, Haggai, and John the Baptist were incarnate angels. This tradition is not accepted in scholarly circles today, if, indeed, it ever was considered seriously. Other possible identifications of the one called "my messenger" in Malachi have been suggested. The Targum of Jonathan, the Talmud, many Rabbis, and some Church Fathers regard Ezra to be the author.[2] Mordecai, Zerubbabel, Haggai, and Nehemiah also have been considered as possible identifications of the one called "Malachi."

Another evidence of the fact that the book should be

[1] See George Buchanan Gray, *A Critical Introduction to the Old Testament* (New York: Charles Scribner's Sons, 1913), p. 231; "Malachi," *Dictionary of the Bible*, 1965, p. 537; Robert H. Pfeiffer, *The Books of the Old Testament* (New York: Harper & Brothers Publishers, 1957), p. 322; and Artur Weiser, *The Old Testament: Its Formation and Development* (New York: Association Press, 1963), p. 275.

[2] Cf. F. W. Farrar, *The Minor Prophets* (New York: Fleming H. Revell Company, n.d.), p. 223; and Eli Cashdan, "Malachi," *The Twelve Prophets*, ed. by A. Cohen (Bournemouth: The Soncino Press, 1948), p. 335.

considered anonymous is that the last six chapters of Zechariah and the book of Malachi originally were considered to be three anonymous documents or oracles comprising an appendix to the Book of the Twelve. A mark of striking similarity in these materials is the appearance of the term "the burden of the word of the Lord" in the first verse of each of these oracles (cf. Zech. 9:1; 12:1; Mal. 1:1). This phrase is not found in these exact words anywhere else in the Old Testament. It is suggested that these chapters were at one time made a part of the book of Zechariah, and later Malachi was separated from them to form the last book of the minor prophets in order to have twelve books.

Although the preceding arguments should be taken seriously, it must be observed that there are some excellent scholars who are not convinced by them. Sellin declared that Malachi "stands before us on the ground of his book as a clear-cut and characteristic personality." [1] Cartledge supports the view "that Malachi was intended to be the actual name of the prophet." [2] Recognizing some problems relative to the authorship of Malachi and admitting that there may "be some legitimacy for the view that regards the work as an anonymous composition," R. K. Harrison considers Malachi to be the name of the author. [3] George Adam Smith said, "It is true that neither in form nor in meaning is there any insuperable obstacle to our understanding 'male 'akhi,' as the name of a person." [4] Some

---

[1] E. Sellin, *Introduction to the Old Testament*, trans. by W. Montgomery (London: Hodder and Stoughton, Limited, 1923), p. 193.

[2] Samuel A. Cartledge, *A Conservative Introduction to the Old Testament* (Grand Rapids: Zondervan Publishing House, 1943), p. 164.

[3] R. K. Harrison, *Introduction to the Old Testament* (Grand Rapids: William B. Eerdmans Publishing Company, 1969), p. 958.

[4] George Adam Smith, *The Book of the Twelve Prophets*, Vol. II (New and revised ed.; London: Hodder and Stoughton, 1928), p. 323.

interpreters regard the name as a shortened form of Malachiah, which is translated "messenger of Yahweh."

Accepting Malachi, however, as properly the name of the prophet, we may not improbably regard it as an abbreviated form of Malachiah, "the messenger of Jehovah," just as Abi is, we know, the equivalent of Abiah, and Uri has been thought to be an abbreviation of Uriah.[1]

This would be parallel to the names of other Hebrew prophets such as Obadiah, Micaiah, Isaiah, Jeremiah, and Zechariah. It is to be noted that the name Malachiah is found in Jeremiah 21:1. Another reason for accepting the word Malachi as a personal name is that none of the other prophetical books is anonymous, and it would be a strange exception for this book to be regarded as such. T. Miles Bennett declared:

Furthermore, 2 Esdras, dating from the second century A.D. but representing a much older tradition, lists the twelve minor prophets, naming as the last three "Haggai, Zechariah, and Malachi, who is also called the angel (messenger) of the Lord" (1:40). By the second century A.D. numerous versions of the Scripture considered Malachi as a proper name (see versions of Aquila, Symmachus, and Theodotion).[2]

The evidence which has been presented is sufficient to warrant the acceptance of Malachi as a proper noun, a suitable name for a Jewish lad, and the author of the otherwise nameless book which closes the Old Testament canon. It is in reality an appropriate name for every true prophet of Yahweh. Even those who consider "Malachi" as a title find themselves virtually saying, "if Malachi is not the name of the prophet, it ought to be."

If the reader has lingering questions regarding the identity of the author of this significant book, he might observe that the trustworthiness of the message and its right to a place in the

---

[1] T. T. Perowne, *Malachi, with Notes and Introduction*, The Cambridge Bible for Schools and Colleges (Cambridge: University Press, 1896), p. 7.

[2] T. Miles Bennett, "Malachi," *The Broadman Bible Commentary*, ed. by Clifton J. Allen, Vol. VII (Nashville: Broadman Press, 1972), p. 367.

Bible have not been questioned, not even by scholars who unhesitatingly declare that the book is anonymous. Thus the book is to be accepted as the Word of God just as much as any other part of the biblical record, even if the author is thought to be unknown (cf. Joshua, Judges, Ruth, Samuel, Kings, Chronicles and many of the Psalms). If, indeed, the prophet who preached and wrote what is found in this book is unknown, it well may be that a marker should be erected to his memory that would read, "to the unknown prophet, symbolic of all such prophets who came before him, and all who shall follow in his train."

The date of Malachi is as much a problem for interpreters as is the identity of the author. The dates suggested range all the way from 525 to 300 B.C. No date can be determined with absolute certainty. The major source of information is internal, and it does not provide a definite answer. The prevailing opinion, however, is that the pendulum swings from the middle of the fifth century to ca. 430 B.C. The Jews had returned to their native land and were under a governor (cf. 1:8). The temple was completed in the time of Zerubbabel, Haggai, and Zechariah ca. 516 B.C. Worship at the temple in the time of Malachi was being observed in such a slovenly and slavish manner as to suggest that some years had passed since its completion (cf. Ezra 6:16-18). The Edomites had been driven from their land (cf. 1:21). This makes the above date which is suggested for Malachi highly probable. Malachi may have appeared shortly before the time of Nehemiah ca. 450 B.C. This conclusion is based on the supposition that the name of Nehemiah would have been given if Malachi had been written while Nehemiah was governor of Judah (cf. Mal. 1:8; Neh. 5:15-18). It must be observed that this conclusion is not accepted by many critical scholars, because it is an argument from silence.

Serious consideration must be given to the fact that some of the problems which plagued Malachi, such as worship, marital fidelity, and tithes and offerings, also are considered by Ezra and Nehemiah. Therefore, it is reasonable to conclude that they either were contemporaries or not far removed with respect to chronology and events. Whatever method is employed to arrive at a date, this fact that Malachi's problems were similar to those of Ezra and Nehemiah seems decisive. This would mean that the dates 450-430 B.C. are as accurate and as acceptable as any.

THE POST-EXILIC COMMUNITY IN THE TIME OF MALACHI

The time in which Malachi exercised his ministry must be described if his message and ministry are to be interpreted, and if the moods, manner, and motivation of the messenger are to be understood.

The political climate must have been comparable to that which prevailed in the time of Sheshbazzar and Zerubbabel, the Jews' governors in the latter part of the sixth century B.C. when they first returned from captivity (cf. Ezra 3:1-6:15). This is a valid conclusion because they were still under the control of the Persian government which continued up to 332 B.C. It appears that they were given rather generous freedom with respect to home rule, customs, and religion, although they were ruled by a governor who was appointed by the Persians. It is significant that Nehemiah served two separate terms as governor.

In spite of the fact that they enjoyed much freedom and favor as a subject people, they were subjected to the hardships of taxation, military occupation, and levies of soldiers for the Persian military. The Persian government had a special garrison that kept watch over her captive people. It was their responsibility to report any strange movements that could be considered as subversive acts. Tettenai was in charge of this garrison among the Jews and maintained oversight at the time of the rebuilding of the temple (cf. Ezra 5:3ff). The Samaritans perhaps brought pressure to bear on this satrap to get work on the temple stopped.

It should be apparent that the governors of Israel had the power and ability to govern. This conclusion is based on the fact that they were appointed by the Persian government. This was the basis of their allegiance and their establishment of certain governmental policies and restrictions. It also was the guarantee of surveillance and the power to govern. It is evident that the governors were respected by the people over whom they exercised authority (cf. Mal. 1:8). They were accepted, and it may be that some of them were believed to be ordained and empowered of God. It is probable that Zerubbabel was regarded as the fulfillment of the prophecy concerning the coming of David as their prince (cf. Jer. 30:9; Ezek. 34:24; 37:24; Hosea 3:5; Hag. 2:20-23; Zech. 4:6-10). The above conclusions are further strengthened by the fact that there are no accounts of rebellions and uprisings against the government recorded by Malachi. The rulers apparently ruled with reasonable justice.

The religious situation of the post-exilic community also is of major importance to God's prophet and to the interpreter. Much of Israel's religious history could be viewed with justifiable pride. This is particularly applicable to a faithful remnant of new covenant people who were the true citizens of Zion. Many of the people who went into captivity were of sturdy stock. They kept the covenant of Yahweh, suffered chastisement for their sin, and refused to let the hope of Israel die in their households. Regarding the faith of these captives, Bright said, "Hope could not die in Israel, because hope was integral to faith, and faith was indestructable."[1]

Thus the roots of religious vitality which provided the foundation and an element of stability for the new community in Judah reach all the way back to the exile. The preaching and ministry of Jeremiah could never be forgotten by those captives over whom he wept, for whom he prayed, to whom he proclaimed God's message, and to whom he wrote after they were taken away (cf. 8:21-9:1; 20:8-9; 29:1ff.). Ezekiel joined Jeremiah in helping the people to interpret their sufferings as God's chastisement for their sins. This did not remove the suffering, but it gave them a weapon with which to fight, and strength, determination, and faith to endure. They were as

---

[1] John Bright, *The Kingdom of God* (Nashville: Abingdon-Cokesbury Press, 1953), p. 134.

those who beheld him who is invisible and the author and finisher of their faith (cf. Heb. 12:2).

Unfortunately, Malachi did not see and experience the glow and glory of the temple nor the exuberance of some of the people when it was erected (cf. Ezra 6:16-18). When he began to exercise his ministry, the clouds of pessimism and cynicism had hovered over the mountains and settled down upon the valleys of the religious community. Worship had ceased to be a delight; it had become either a distasteful duty or a bitter dose. Yahweh's government of the world was considered by many people to be impotent. "The wicked," they said, "fared better than the righteous; there was no such thing as a God of justice" (cf. 2:17). It was the age-old complaint that the wicked prosper and that the righteous suffer (cf. 3:13-15; Ps. 73:3ff.; Jer. 12:1f.; Hab. 1:2-11).

Unacceptable offerings were brought to the Lord which profaned his altar. But the spirit and attitude of the people were even more unacceptable than their offerings. The Lord cried out for someone to close the doors of the temple and to put a stop to the corrupt, hypocritical worship (cf. 1:7-10). Pagan living and idolatry were gaining strength in the land. Home life was corrupted by intermarriage with idolatrous worshipers (cf. 2:10-12; Ezra 10:2; Neh. 13:23-27). The people who were called on to reckon with their origin as a nation and to magnify their distinctives as God's covenant people provided a strange burlesque.

The principles of the religion of Israel which had been shaken or obscured by the delinquency of the people during the half-century after the rebuilding of the Temple were three—the the distinctive Love of Yahweh for His people, His Holiness, and His Righteousness. "Malachi" takes up each of these in turn, and proves or enforces it according as the people have formally doubted it or in their carelessness done it despite.[1]

The time was marked by economic depression. On account of this, the people had become cynical and hard to entreat. God's tithes and offerings were being withheld, bringing about the necessity for more severe chastisements, and causing limitations

---

[1] Smith, *The Book of the Twelve Prophets*, pp. 340-41.

and hardships for the religious institutions and those who served them (cf. 3:2-4, 6-8).

THE PERSON OF THE PROPHET

The only data which are available regarding Malachi are in the book which bears his name. There is much to be desired, however, in the quest of information about the person of the prophet even in this source. The word "prophet" is not used, and no account is given of a vision of God or of a dramatic call to be the messenger of Yahweh (cf. Isa. 6:1-9; Jer. 1:4-10; Ezek. 2:1-7; Amos 7:14). It is not even declared that the word of the Lord came to him (cf. Hosea 1:1; Joel 1:1; Jonah 1:1; Zeph. 1:1). Nothing is said about Malachi's parents, his birth place, family life, occupation, or personal experiences. That he lived and preached in Jerusalem is a valid assumption. His ancient peer, Elijah, had descended on his generation with very much of the same mystery, message, and manner.

The problems about the identity of Malachi and the limited data from which to gather information, however, should not close the door of research. One should not conclude that it is futile to seek any information or to gain helpful insights regarding his person and work. If this premise should be accepted and followed with regard to Joel, Obadiah, Nahum, Habakkuk, and Zephaniah, it would be logical to judge any effort to gather trustworthy information regarding them to be an unprofitable pursuit. This same logic could be applied with regard to a study of other biblical characters and in other areas of research, biblical and non-biblical.

As one reads the book of Malachi, certain valid conclusions can be drawn regarding the person of the prophet. He is a genuine prophet and worthy to bear the name. He feared God, honored the governor-king, grieved over abuses in worship, marital infidelity, and social injustice. Unique mental, emotional, and spiritual endowments are readily evident. His ability to face the tough questions and to debate the issues which were hurled at him by the "Epicurean" cynics to whom he preached and with whom he debated mark him as intellectually competent, a man of unusual perceptions and keen insights (cf. 1:2-5). His emotions were stirred and moved to great depths as he preached the love of God, faced the people with their sin, entreated them to repent, and looked to the triumph of the Lord and his cause (cf. 3:4, 17; 4:2). Spiritual qualities such as the knowledge of God, faith, love, righteousness, righteous indignation, and faithfulness are evident in the life and ministry of this courageous prophet of God. It is because of these endowments that he was not overwhelmed by his problems nor intimidated by his cynical, irreligious foes.

He is God's messenger. The meaning of his name is significant at this point. The message which he proclaimed is the word of Yahweh. He may be seen as a religious news analyst who seeks to gather and interpret news as it relates to the world of religion. He has serious pronouncements to make regarding worship and religious leadership. He carefully scrutinizes and analyzes the attitudes and participation of the worshippers. He condemns their sin. His call to repentance is loud and clear. This marks him as the master diagnostician who was able to look beneath the outward forms of ritual and "religiosity" and to uncover the sordid, festering sores of spiritual corruption that were the real cause of their trouble. He also knows that both a balm and a physician are available for healing and restoration to spiritual health and vitality (cf. Jer. 8:22).

He acts out the role of a serious student of history who seeks to read the signs of the times as he endeavors to deal with the nations and especially with Israel. In this he knows that they are Yahweh's covenant people who are failing to keep the covenant and inviting the judgment of the Almighty (cf. 2:8-9; Ex. 19:5-6; Amos 3:2). The providence of the Lord in world affairs is emphasized. His name is reverenced among the nations and his kingship is magnified (cf. 1:11, 14). This is made prominent by the fact that the Lord used a heathen power as a chastening scourge to punish Israel's sins, and he raised up another power to work his work of a new exodus to bring his people back to their land.

Finally, Malachi may be judged as a preacher of no mean

ability. He insisted on the personal and spiritual aspects of Yahweh worship. His arguments in preaching were strengthened by historical proofs, the demands of the Levitical Code, the Law of Moses, and the promise of rewards and punishments in the Day of Yahweh.

DISTINCTIVE FEATURES OF THE BOOK OF MALACHI

In considering the distinctive features of the book of Malachi, the prophet's style must be valued as one of its unique qualities. Robinson declared:

His style is doubtless inferior to that of some of the pre-exilic prophets, yet he possesses a vigor and force which they seldom surpass. Occasionally he reveals touches of prophetic imagination worthy of his predecessors; even poetic rhythm and parallelism (cf. 1:11; 3:1, 6, 10; 4:1). His figures are always chaste and beautiful (cf. 1:6; 3:2, 3; 4:1-3).[1]

The language is predominantly prose with only a trace of poetry. It is forceful and direct, carefully planned and systematically arranged. This is seen in the choice of vocabulary, historical perspective, and forensic qualities. It is a single unit with a central theme, the work of a single mind. Robinson said of Malachi: "He shows clearly the influence of the schools, and is on the way to the Talmud."[2]

This book has been appropriately characterized as didactic and dialectical. Robinson referred to the prophet as "Malachi the Lecturer."[3] The use of the interrogative, magnifying the question and answer method in determined debate, distinguishes the significant and logically arranged feature of the style. It reveals that Malachi was a logician and a hard hitting debater. It is this feature that provoked Robinson to say that

---

[1] George L. Robinson, *The Twelve Minor Prophets* (New York: George H. Dorian Company, 1926), p. 160.

[2] *Ibid.*, p. 162.

[3] *Ibid.*

"his (Malachi's) book may be fairly classed as the most argumentative of all Old Testament prophecies."[1] This is distinguished and dramatically emphasized by the prophet's declaration of a fact, the retort of his hearers with a question that is a cynical repudiation of the declaration, and the response of the prophet in a further clarification of the previously declared fact. There are eight examples of these dialogues or points of debate interspersed throughout the book. They are easily identified by the characteristic and recurring phrase "yet you say, 'wherein?' " This term is used in 1:2, 6, 7; 2:14, 17; 3:7, 8, 13. The people talked back to the prophet as they did in Jeremiah's time, perhaps in a more cynical and aggressive manner. These emphases will receive further consideration in the treatment of the text.

Antecedents of this method can be detected in the proclamations of Amos, Jeremiah, Ezekiel, Haggai, and Zechariah. It may be said to have come to its fullest flower in the time of Malachi. This in part accounts for the fact that the office of the prophet was considered to be in transition in the time of Malachi. This in part accounts for the fact that the office of the prophet was considered to be in transition in the time of Malachi from that of proclaimer to the role of teacher. This method is found also in the distinctive teaching techniques employed by the Greek philosopher Socrates. This is the reason that Robinson called Malachi "the Hebrew Socrates."[2] George Adam Smith has concluded:

> Just as with Zephaniah we saw prophecy into apocalypse, and with Habakkuk into the speculation of the schools of wisdom, so now in "Malachi" we perceive it tending towards the scholasticism of the Rabbis.[3]

Malachi is the forerunner of later Judaism. The synagogue and other schools in Israel after the time of Malachi employed this method of teaching.

---

[1] *Ibid.*

[2] *Ibid.*, p. 161.

[3] Smith, *The Book of the Twelve Prophets*, p. 337.

Malachi: Messenger of Divine Love

Some other features of the book should be considered. It is placed in the Old Testament as the last book of the canon, although it probably is not the last book that was written. It is brief: there are only fifty-five verses divided into four chapters. (The Hebrew or Masoretic text has only three chapters.) Verses 1:3, 11; 2:2, 10-15; 3:1, 10-12; 4:3, 5-6 constitute the more difficult portions of the book. They are both a problem and a challenge for the interpreter.

There is a great historical significance in Malachi because it is a most important biblical source of information about the life and times of the post-exilic community in Jerusalem following the time of Haggai and Zechariah up to and including the period of Ezra and Nehemiah. Indeed, the spirit and some of the proclamations in the book of Malachi have much in common with Ezra and Nehemiah. There is a manifest nostalgia for the "good old days" of Yahweh's work among his people (cf. 2:4-7; 3:7-12; Hab. 3:2). The book is marked by a strong apocalyptic tone and by a messianic emphasis on the coming of a divine deliverer (cf. 3:13-4:2).

Ordinary or characteristic Judaism is reflected in the attitude toward Edom (cf. 1:2), concern for a pure ritual (cf. 3:4), and the apocalyptic emphases (cf. 3:1-2; 4:1-6). The personal and spiritual aspects of true religion are focused. Arguments in preaching were strengthened by historical data (cf. 1:2-5), the demands of the Levitical Code (cf. 1:7-9, 12-14), the law of Moses (cf. 2:7-8; 2:17-3:12; 4:4), and the promise of rewards and punishments in the Day of Yahweh (cf. 4:1-3). Farrar, with keen insight, has observed:

> Already we see in Malachi the germs of Pharisaism which relied on mere external ordinances; of the Sadduceeism, which minimized the elements of religious faith; and of the open worldliness which cared for nothing but the greed and the lusts of the present life.[1]

It is to be observed that some things are not found in Malachi which have a degree of prominence in the other books of the prophets. There is no mention of a king, only a governor (cf. 1:8; Isa. 1:1; Jer. 1:2-3; Hosea 1:1; Amos 1:1). There is no

---

[1] Farrar, *The Minor Prophets*, p. 225.

record of a vision of God either in the account of the prophet's call or in his message. (Contrast with Isa. 6:1ff; Jer. 1:11ff.; Ezek. 1:4ff; Amos 7:1ff.). No reference is made to the Spirit of God (cf. Isa. 63:10; Ezek. 2:2; Micah 3:8; Joel 2:28-29; Zech. 4:6). There are no oracles against foreigners.

THE MESSAGE AND THEOLOGY OF MALACHI

The message and theology of Malachi magnify the great themes of the Bible. The loftiest emphasis which is made is the love of God for his people. "I have loved you" is one of the most profound and amazing declarations in all the Bible (cf. 1:2). This is the theme of Malachi. He emphasizes the fact that this love is universal, absolute, articulate, providential, and enduring. Herein the messenger of divine love unveils his portrait of God as a loving father who yearns for his prodigal son as he seeks to reclaim him (1:2-5). He points to the barricades which hinder the operation of his love (1:6-3:12), and declares that it will be fully experienced in the day of Yahweh (3:13-4:6). The preaching of the prophet is the old story of love that is often unappreciated and unappropriated, but is always unrelenting in its objectives. This aspect of God's character will be considered further in the exegesis of the text.

God's blessings upon his people and his purpose for them are evaluated and emphasized. Thus they are confronted with their responsibility as the elect of God and a kingdom of priests in which faith and obedience are magnified with a view to the ultimate goal of a holy nation (cf. 3:16-18; Gen. 12:1-3; Ex. 19:4-6).

Deity is uniquely presented and characterized throughout the fifty-five verses of the book by the use of several different terms. The most prominent term which is employed is "Yahweh of hosts." It is used twenty-four times; Yahweh, twenty-one times; God, nine times; Lord, once; Father, twice; and Master and King, one time each.

"My Name," designating Yahweh, is prominent. The priests are charged with despising his Name by offering polluted offerings on his altar (cf. 1:6). His Name is made great among the heathen by their offering incense and a pure offering to the Lord and by their reverence of him (cf. 1:11, 14). A curse is threatened against those who do not give glory to or magnify the Name (cf. 2:1-2). Those who reverenced the Lord and thought on his Name were heard by him. They were included in his book of remembrance as his special possession and his faithful sons (cf. 3:16-17). In the day of the Lord when judgment comes, those who fear the Name will be blessed by the rising of the sun of righteousness with healing in its wings (cf. 4:1-2).

In addition to the above distinctive terms and sometimes in association with them, God is presented as one to be honored and reverenced (cf. 1:6). He is the covenant maker (cf. 2:4) and creator (cf. 2:10). He is declared to be the owner of the sanctuary and the altar (cf. 2:11, 13); one who hates divorce and is wearied by empty words (cf. 2:16-17). He is portrayed as a refiner and purifier (cf. 3:3), the judge (cf. 3:5), and the unchangeable one (cf. 3:6).

Sin is dealt with in a forthright manner. It is confronted by reference to the love of Yahweh, a call to repentance, the faithfulness of a remnant of a previous generation, and the promise of forgiveness and blessing to every believer. Some of the sins which the prophet names are sorcery, adultery, lying, oppression of the wage earner, wrong treatment of widows, orphans, and foreigners, and the failure to reverence God (cf. 3:5). The law of Moses and the Levitical Code are utilized as standards of measurements, principles of morality and righteousness, and the basis and character of judgment on impenitent sinners.

Other key emphases are the universality of Yahweh worship (cf. 1:11), national unity and equality (cf. 2:10), chastisement for sin, and the day of Yahweh which anticipates judgment, cleansing, and new life (cf. 3:3, 5, 8; 4:1ff.). Malachi is further distinguished by a strong Deuteronomic emphasis (cf. 1:8; 2:11; 3:8-10; 4:4). The references to the priests as sons of Levi (cf. 3:3) and Horeb (cf. 4:4) reflect the Deuteronomic Code. The Priestly Code uses sons of Aaron and Sinai. The teaching concerning divorce and remarriage, although predominantly patriarchal in its application, is closer to the concept of Jesus and the New Testament than that of any other Old Testament prophet who deals with this subject (cf. 2:13-16).

Emphasis on worship in Israel is paramount. Leadership in this important phase of the people's lives is provided by priests, Levites, and the prophet himself. The temple and the sacrificial system are given unusual prominence in the book. Watts said:

The Temple symbolizes the kingdom of God. It is the throne room of the Lord. Its rituals explain and proclaim the kingdom. Its gatherings are opportunities to experience and celebrate the kingdom. [1]

The prophet preached a sermon to the priests in which he magnified the faithfulness of Levi, the responsibilities of the priests, the failure of the backsliders among them in his time, and the judgment of God which was being visited upon them (cf. 2:4-9). It is evident that he had no sympathy for the corrupt priests and the farce of formalism which was being practiced in worship.

Theodicy is dominant in Malachi's defense against the sharp accusations which are made by the people concerning the justice of the Lord (cf. 2:17; 3:13-15). The answers which are given to their charges magnify the sin of the people (cf. 1:6-2:9; 3:5-12). They conform to the Deuteronomic pattern which pervades the book. These concepts are prominent in the arguments of Job's friends, the blessing and the curse in Deuteronomy 28, portions of the book of Proverbs, Jeremiah 12, and Psalms 37 and 73. The witnesses who are called to the stand by Malachi are Jacob and Esau (cf. 1:2-5). The blessing of Jacob is magnified, while the curse is being visited upon Esau. The final emphasis is given in the language of apocalypticism, in which the ultimate defeat of evil and the triumph of righteousness prevail (cf. 3:16-4:3). Although his ways are past finding out and he is accused falsely, God remains just and justified in his conduct of

---

[1] John D. W. Watts, "Zechariah," *The Broadman Bible Commentary*, ed. by Clifton J. Allen, Vol. VII (Nashville: Broadman Press, 1972), p. 311.

the affairs of the world in Malachi's vindication. [1]

The covenant is made prominent, and in some ways unique, throughout the book. First, there is a covenant with Levi which is said to have been corrupted (cf. 2:9). Second, the covenant of the fathers is profaned (cf. 2:10). Third, a covenant existed between husband and wife. The wife is said to be a covenant companion against whom the husband is accused of being faithless (cf. 2:14-15). Fourth, the messenger of the covenant is introduced as a coming one in whom the people are said to delight. He is pictured as awesome and as a refiner and purifier of the sons of Levi (cf. 3:1-3). Fifth, the whole worship system is associated with the covenant. The temple and the ritual constituted a place and a means by which the worshippers maintained and strengthened their covenant obligations. Although they knew the importance of the political, religious, and economic structures of Israel, the prophets view their history theologically in covenantal relationships. This was prominent in their preaching as they besought the nation to renew her covenant vows. The old order was condemned, and its doom was near (cf. Zeph. 1:14). [2]

Malachi's emphasis on the true value of ritual (cf. 1:6ff.), the crime of divorce (cf. 2:10ff.), the coming of the Messiah and his kingdom (cf. 3:1ff.), and the eternal discipline of the Law (cf. 4:4-6) are considered by Robinson to be the prophet's major points in preparing the way for the coming of the Messiah. [3]

The message and theology of Malachi are strengthened and enhanced by the references to the book which are found in the New Testament (cf. Matt. 11:10, 17:12; Mark 1:2; 9:11; Luke 1:17; Jno. 1:21; Rom. 9:13).

[1] Robert C. Dentan, "The Book of Malachi," *The Interpreter's Bible*, ed. by George A. Buttrick, Vol. VI (Nashville: Abingdon Press, 1956), pp. 1119-1120.

[2] R. B. Y. Scott, *The Relevance of the Prophets* (New York: The Macmillan Company, 1957), pp. 177-78.

[3] Robinson, *The Twelve Minor Prophets*, pp. 165-69.

OUTLINE OF THE BOOK

I. Divine Love Declared (1:1-5)
   A. The superscription (1:1)
   B. The proclamation of divine love by Yahweh (1:2a)
   C. Divine love declared in visitation upon the cynical (1:2b)
   D. Divine love declared in contrasted dealings with Jacob and Esau (1:2c-5)

II. Divine Love Dishonored (1:6-14)
   A. The fact of dishonored love (1:6a)
   B. The denial of dishonored love (1:6b)
   C. The means by which love is dishonored (1:7-8)
   D. The curse of dishonored love (1:9-14)
      1. God's favor is withdrawn (1:9)
      2. It makes worship at the temple unacceptable (1:10)
      3. God is turning to others who honor him (1:11)
      4. God's name is profaned and their way is cursed (1:12-14)

III. Divine Love Threatens Punishment (2:1-9)
   A. The declaration that divine love threatens punishment (2:1-3)
      1. An entreaty to repent (2:1-2a)
      2. The punishment described (2:2b-3)
         a) Blessings are to be cursed (2:2b)
         b) Disqualified for service (2:3)
   B. The commandment and the covenant emphasized (2:4-5)
   C. Reverence and obedience magnified (2:6-7)
   D. Punishment justified (2:8-9)

IV. Divine Love Despises Unfaithfulness (2:10-17)
   A. Unfaithfulness defined (2:10-11)
      1. Profaning the covenant of the fathers (2:10)
      2. Profaning the sanctuary of the Lord (2:11)
   B. Unfaithfulness to meet with severity (2:12-17)
      1. The guilty to be cut off (2:12)
      2. Offerings to be rejected (2:13)

      3. The work of Yahweh the God of justice (2:14-17)
        a) Witnessing wrong doing (2:14)
        b) Desiring godly offspring (2:15)
        c) Condemning divorce and skepticism (2:16-17)
  V. Divine Love Personally Manifested (3:1-6)
    A. Through the messenger of the covenant (3:1)
      1. His coming to be heralded by his messenger (3:1a)
      2. The messenger of the covenant is the Lord himself (3:1b)
    B. By severe purging (3:2-6)
      1. Creating fear (3:2-3a)
      2. Involving the sons of Levi (3:3b-4)
      3. Condemning specific sins (3:5)
      4. Sparing a remnant (3:6)
 VI. Divine Love Demands Obedience (3:7-12)
    A. Involving ordinances long disobeyed (3:7-12)
    B. The call to return (3:7b)
    C. The call to return is spurned (3:7c)
    D. Obedience involves the tithe (3:8)
    E. The curse of disobedience (3:9)
    F. The blessings of obedience (3:10-12)
VII. Divine Love Expressed in Righteous Judgment (3:13-4:6)
    A. God-fearers complain (3:13-16a)
    B. God-fearers remembered by Yahweh as his own possession (3:16b-17)
    C. Approval and acceptance of the discriminating sentence (3:18)
    D. Destruction of the wicked (4:1)
    E. Preservation of the godly (4:2-3)

Conclusion: Law and prophecy to be utilized to bring the nation to God before he strikes in judgment (4:4-6)

II. Divine Love Declared

THE SUPERSCRIPTION (1:1)

1:1 The burden of the word of Yahweh unto Israel by the hand of Malachi. [1]

The superscriptions or titles of the books of the prophets are given in the opening verse or verses. In some cases unusually significant materials are provided (cf. Isa. 1:1; Jer. 1:1-3; Ezek. 1:1-3; Hos. 1:1; Amos 1:1-2). In other instances only one sentence is given, providing very limited data (cf. Joel 1:1; Nah. 1:1; Hab. 1:1). The latter is the case with Malachi.

There is general agreement among interpreters that the title of Malachi is a contribution of a scribe or an editor and was not

[1] The written text of Malachi which is used in this work is the author's translation of the third edition of the Hebrew text of *Biblia Hebraica*. All other scripture references will be taken from the text of the Revised Standard Version unless otherwise indicated.

written by the prophet himself. This same opinion prevails with respect to other books of the prophets. The significant thing, however, is not the origin of these titles, but the information which is provided. This is a helpful key in unlocking the book, even though concern is sometimes expressed relative to the origin and accuracy of the information which is given. The title verse of Malachi gives the character of the message, its source, the people to whom it is directed, and the agent by whom it is delivered.

The burden is stated. The word "burden" is a translation of *masa* , a passive participle, from the Hebrew verb form meaning "to lift up," "to bear," or "to carry." The term "burden" appears to be used distinctively and at crucial junctures in prophetic proclamations (cf. Isa. 13:1; 14:28; 15:1; 17:1; 19:1; Hab. 1:1; Nah. 1:1; Zech. 9:1; 12:1). It is found also in Proverbs 30:1 and 31:1. As it is used in messages of the prophets, the translation "lift up," signifying the lifting up of the voice in proclaiming or preaching, seems to convey its basic meaning. In common usage, it is sometimes translated by the words "oracle," "word," or "message." Its specific use is regarded as a means of introducing a prophetic message against rebellious sinners, which is a fearful threat of judgment. Its use by the prophets is distinctive and easily verified. It is the most severe term which is used to designate prophecy. Thus it was both a burden, a weighty message, to the prophet who proclaimed it, and to the people to whom and against whom it was proclaimed. This marks its restricted and unique usage. An examination of the texts where it is used will bear this out.

In considering the word "burden," Moore declared:

It is always prefixed to prophecies of a threatening character, and seems designed to indicate the fact, that like some dark cloud, heavy with its pent-up fury, these prophecies are surcharged with the wrath of God, and hang ready to pour their dreadful contents on those against whom they are directed.[1]

[1] T. V. Moore, *The Prophets of the Restoration* (New York: Robert Carter and Brothers, 1856), p. 337.

The phrase "of the word of Yahweh" declares that the message which the prophet proclaimed came from the Lord; indeed it is God's word (cf. Hos. 1:1; Joel 1:1; Jonah 1:1; Mic. 1:1; Zeph. 1:1). There is no explanation of the means by which the word came. In some cases prophets received a communication from the Lord by a vision, a dream, or an experience in life (cf. Isa. 6:1ff.; Ezek. 1:1ff.; Gen. 15:12ff.; Hos. 1:2ff.). The important thing, however, is not how, but that the message came; it was from the Lord, and it was heard and proclaimed.

"Yahweh," sometimes translated "LORD" with four capital letters (KJV and RSV) and "Jehovah" (ASV), is the personal name of God. "Yahweh" will be used throughout this work, not as a substitute for the name of deity, but as a means of emphasizing it, and as an effort to recapture what appears to be a transliteration of its nearest Hebrew equivalent. Its use follows a widely accepted practice among Old Testament scholars today. This word is significant in the call of Moses (cf. Ex. 3:1ff.). Its proclamation and clear enunciation are given in the renewal of the covenant (cf. Ex. 34:6-7). This makes it distinctive. The later use of "the Name" became the foundation of the preaching of all the Hebrew prophets. It is used almost exclusively in Malachi. Additional information and further references are available.[1]

"Unto Israel" specifies the people to whom the message is directed. Some prophetic proclamations are directed to other nations (cf. Isa. 13-23; Jer. 46-51; Ezek. 25-32). Most of the preaching of the prophets, however, was to Israel as a whole or to groups and individuals within the nation. Malachi refers to Edom and to heathen people in general, but such references were for the purpose of strengthening his message to Israel.

---

[1] See Robert S. Cripps, *A Critical and Exegetical Commentary on the Book of Amos* (reprint ed.; London: S.P.C.K., 1969), pp. 327ff.; Robert Baker Girdlestone, *Synonyms of the Old Testament* (Grand Rapids: Wm. B. Eerdmans Publishing Co., 1948), pp. 45-54; and J. Wash Watts, *A Distinctive Translation of Genesis* (Grand Rapids: Wm. B. Eerdmans Publishing Co., 1963), pp. 136-38.

Malachi: Messenger of Divine Love

The name Israel is significant in the history of this people. The first instance of its use is when the Lord changed the name of Jacob to Israel (cf. Gen. 32:28). It may mean "one who strives with God" or "a prince of God." In a strict application of the term, it could be said that Jacob-Israel became the father of the people of Israel. After the division of the twelve tribes, the people of the ten northern tribes were called Israel. The two tribes, Judah and Benjamin, comprising the southern kingdom, were known as Judah. After the return from Babylonian captivity, all of the Hebrew people were referred to as Israel, because the two kingdoms no longer existed (cf. Ezra 7:10). They were Israelites and not Moabites, Ammonites, or Edomites.

"By the hand of Malachi" has attracted as much attention in scholarly circles as any part of the book of Malachi. The name or term "Malachi" has been discussed in the introductory portion of this commentary. Even though it has been regarded as a title by many interpreters, it has become an acceptable name for the author. No one ever refers to this book simply as the last book of the Old Testament or the last book of the prophets. If an editor took the word Malachi from 3:1 and put it back in 1:1, it appears that he regarded it as an appropriate means of identifying the book. Whatever may be concluded from as to the identity of the prophet, it is evident that there is in this book a message from Yahweh and someone to proclaim it.

The opening verses of this book constitute a mountain peak upon which the interpreter may stand to gaze upon the glorious past of divine revelation. From this vantage point, one may see the time of the prophet and its responsibility for all that has been thrust upon it and all that could come from it. One may look to the future with anticipation and hope. One may also hear the law, all the prophets who have gone before, and the psalmists as they speak and sing of the great God of the universe whose dominating attribute is love. As one looks to the present, one must find God's purpose for him in relationship to the revelation which God makes.

The prospects of the unfolding future declare that there is even more, for the love of God awaits a personal embodiment in the flesh both to declare and to demonstrate the eternal truth that God is love. Thus Malachi is the bridge between the two great covenants of Moses and Christ which are united in one in the dominating theme of divine love.

THE PROCLAMATION OF DIVINE LOVE
BY YAHWEH (1:2a)

1:2a "I have loved you," says Yahweh.

This theme of the book of Malachi, divine love, has roots that reach down into the heart of Yahweh God and branches which extend to all humankind of all time. It is the distinctive of the character of God whereby he is enabled to maintain fellowship with those whom he has created in his image and likeness, even though they rebel against him. None is excluded from this love except the one who refuses to receive it. This latter truth is made a dominant part of Malachi's message as he pleads and debates with his people. It is his purpose both to declare and to illustrate his theme. The foundation is ancient and secure. At first it appears as a spring in the desert, but it is destined to become a mighty river. It flows on even though its fruitage and blessing may not be enjoyed by some because its channels are blocked by their repudiation of it. For those who look to God by faith and fall in love with him, it is a means of cleansing, life, and growth.

It may seem strange to hear the prophet declare the love of God instead of his wrath as he rebukes the people for their sin. His theme prevails, however, because love is the foundational, fundamental message for saints and sinners alike. The word for love which is used by Malachi is expressive of affection that is both human and divine. In the human sphere it includes all of man's desires and relationships, whether pure or impure. Malachi's use of it is to magnify God's magnificent obsession with Israel.

"Have loved" is a previous present verb form in the Hebrew text. It is descriptive of that which reaches back into the past, but it is operative in the present and future. It says, "I have loved you from the beginning, I love you now, and I shall love you." It is on the basis of this love that the prophet condemns Israel's sins, remains steadfast and confident in his preaching, and holds out hope of forgiveness for a penitent people. The love which he declares is that of the eternal God, the creator of the world, the all powerful one, and the redeemer. This is the basis of his choice of Israel when he elected her and set her apart from all others. It is everlasting, unchangeable, unconditional, and sovereign. It is this electing love which is the foundation of the covenant relation between God and his people. This covenant provides the channel of blessing for them and through them to all people (cf. Gen. 12:1-3; Ex. 19:5-6). It is significant that the prevailing use of this word for love in the Old Testament is with reference to the nation of Israel as a whole. It rarely is used to express God's love for individuals. Snaith deals with this word in his discussion of God's election love for Israel. He also discusses the meaning of the word hate as it is applied to Esau.[1] Vriezen has written:

> As for "election," there is no question of arbitrariness, of chance sympathies and antipathies; even when the words love and hatred are used in this connection they are not to be taken in the affective sense; the Hebrew word for "to hate" often means to scorn, or to rank something lower than something else (cf. Deut. xxi. 15) while "to love" may mean to choose something and rank it higher than something else.[2]

Jacob has declared:

> The covenant by which God binds himself to his people—and through his people to humanity as a whole—has profound roots which cannot be defined otherwise than by the mystery of election; but the origin of election is found in love, that is to say in the spontaneous movement which carries one being

[1] Norman H. Snaith, *The Distinctive Ideas of the Old Testament* (London: The Epworth Press, 1944), pp. 131-42.

[2] Th. C. Vriezen, *An Outline of Old Testament Theology* (Oxford: Basil Blackwell, 1958), p. 167.

towards another being with the desire to possess it and to find some satisfaction in that possession.[1]

The theology of these words is to be considered. The essential nature of God is expressed here, because God is love (cf. 1 Jno. 4:8). His love for his people is love with a history. It is the story from of old that can be traced and documented. Indeed, its tracks are the tracks of God. It is emphasized and illustrated at crucial junctures by longsuffering, forbearance, steadfast endurance, and unfailing forgiveness. It is both the secure cornerstone and the strength of the magnificent super-structure of the house which we know as the kingdom of God as it confronts sin. It is that which uncovers and covers. This is the strange paradox of revealing and concealing in the story of redemption. The tender tones in Malachi are of a love that can face sin with a deep yearning for reconciliation, even when that love has been ridiculed and rejected. It is that which seeks to elicit a like response from those who are thus loved. The dominant note of Hebrew faith expressed in Deuteronomy 6:4-7 puts it in these words:

Hear, O Israel: The Lord our God is one Lord;
and you shall love the Lord your God with all your heart, and with all your soul, and with all your might.
And these words which I command you this day shall be upon your heart;
and you shall teach them diligently to your children, and shall talk of them when you sit in your house, and when you walk by the way, and when you lie down, and when you rise.

In Deuteronomy 7:7-11, love is used in a context of God's espousal of Israel (cf. 7:8), signifying their election, deliverance from Egyptian bondage (symbolic of all deliverances), and covenant provisions, which are marked by reciprocal obligations and eternal consequences. A serious warning is sounded, and a vow is declared to visit punishment upon all who hate God, thereby turning away his love. It is emphasized in this context that Israel was not chosen to be God's special people because

---

[1] Edmond Jacob, *Theology of the Old Testament*, trans. by Arthur W. Heathcote and Philip J. Allcock (New York: Harper and Brothers Publishers, 1958), p. 108.

they were greater in number than any other people, but because God loves them (cf. Deut. 26:5-11; Ezek. 16:6-8; Ex. 19:4).

The prophets magnify these profound truths in the unfolding drama of God's dealing with all mankind. The prince of the prophets proclaimed:

I will recount the steadfast love of the Lord, the praises of the Lord, according to all that the Lord has granted us, and the great goodness to the house of Israel which he has granted them according to his mercy, according to the abundance of his steadfast love.

For he said, Surely they are my people, sons who will not deal falsely; and he became their Savior.

In all their affliction he was afflicted, and the angel of his presence saved them; in his love and in his pity he redeemed them; he lifted them up and carried them all the days of old. (Isaiah 63:7-9).

Jeremiah said: "The Lord appeared to him from afar. I have loved you with an everlasting love; therefore I have continued my faithfulness to you" (31:3). The Lord speaks through Hosea, with the emotions and tender memory of a father, saying: "When Israel was a child I loved him and out of Egypt I called my son" (11:1).

That which is declared in the book of Malachi, involving Jacob and Esau, is magnified in the above references. It is particularly emphasized in the passages from Deuteronomy and Isaiah. This love of God, known and experienced throughout Israel's history, is given in simple yet sublime words by Malachi.

With what reception shall these words be met? Surely, the prophet anticipated the kindling of emotions and the expressions of deep gratitude on the part of the people. He is prepared to hear words like those expressed by the psalmist when he ask, "what shall I render to the Lord for all his bounty to me?" (Ps. 116:12). The psalmist seems to say that the greatest that he can do is altogether too little. Then he responds by saying, "I will lift up the cup of salvation and call on the name of the Lord, I will pay my vows to the Lord in the presence of all his people" (116:13-14). This is not what the prophet heard. The response of the people was harsh, disappointing, and unbelievable.

DIVINE LOVE DECLARED AND VISITED
UPON THE CYNICAL (1:2b)

1:2b But you say, "Wherein have you loved us?"
Israel's retort is one of skepticism. The spirit and language
are in the vein of ingratitude and ridicule. It is either verbally
expressed or reflected in their attitude which the prophet puts
in words for them. The question 'Wherein have you loved us?'
is a demand for clarification, by exhibits or examples, of
Yahweh's love.

This unique feature of the style of Malachi which appears at
this point is a characteristic of the book and appears at crucial
junctures in the intermittent dialogue between the prophet and
his hearers. It is the interrogative method which is used in
determined debate with the people. In this series of questions
and answers, sin is condemned, judgment is pronounced, and a
call to repentance is issued. This aspect of the book has been
discussed in the section dealing with introduction.

The response of the people, a virtual denial of the love of
God, which is like that of a father for his son, is comparable to
that which Isaiah described in his song of the vineyard (5:1-4).
The desire of the people for a bill of particulars of the love of
Yahweh to be paraded before them is thought to have been
born of their continuing hardships and sufferings. The fortunes
of the people, including their new temple, were very limited in
comparison to their pre-exilic prosperity and glory, especially in
the eighth century. Also, the promises of prosperity, considered
on a wrong interpretation of the Deuteronomic theology, were
calculated on what could be termed a vending machine basis (cf.
Deut. 7:12-15; 28:1ff.). An input of righteousness, they concluded, was to be rewarded with an output of material
prosperity. It is a lopsided emphasis on the visible and material
rewards of faith. Haggai and Zechariah had made strong
appeals in leading the people to erect the temple. As a reward
for obedience, the people were promised abundant harvests, and
peace and prestige among the nations (cf. Hag. 2:4-9, 20-23;
Zech. 8:9-13).

The temple had been finished for fifty years or longer. The
people had brought their tithes and offerings and observed the

times and seasons of worship with the proper ritual and liturgy. It seemed that the promised blessings from the Lord had been forgotten and would never come. They were still suffering from an economic depression caused by a prolonged drought, pestilence, and crop failure. They continued to be a subject people, dominated by the world's greatest political power. The glowing promises of a new covenant and a new David, indeed, a new regime that would excel the old one in prosperity, peace, and glory had not materialized.

In the face of these undeniable realities, to say that God loved them was considered to be a farce. They were pious and hollow platitudes in which they had no faith. Such promises were counterfeit money. They would not buy clothes and groceries. They were rejected as worthless by the landlord and the tax collector. The people, therefore, exhibit the spirit and attitude which had characterized them from the beginning— ingratitude and murmuring even from the days of their fathers in the wilderness (cf. Ex. 16:2-3; Num. 16:41).

Alas, no one considered that it was because of their sins, which they were too blind to see, that these long hoped for promises were made null and void. Worship that is only outward and formal is not sufficient. Their backslidings and failures are marked by the repudiation of Yahweh. They were guilty of covenant breaking, marital infidelity, robbing God of tithes and offerings, social injustice, and skepticism toward God and all good. It was more comfortable to accuse God of being remiss with respect to his promises than to confess and to repent of their sins. It is reasonable to ponder the enormity of their ingratitude and spiritual blindness that demanded exhibits of the love of God.

It is possible that Malachi desired to use all of his oratory and debating skills in the proclamation of the judgment which was preached by Isaiah to another backslidden generation in the words:

Hear, O heavens, and give ear, O earth;
for the Lord has spoken: "Sons have I
reared and brought up, but they have
rebelled against me.
The ox knows its owner, and the ass its

master's crib; but Israel does not know,
my people does not understand."
Ah, sinful nation, a people laden with
iniquity, offspring of evildoers, sons
who deal corruptly! They have forsaken
the Lord, they have despised the Holy
One of Israel, they are utterly estranged. (Isaiah 1:2-4).

This is not the answer which he gives. The Lord provides an answer for his prophet which is in keeping with the question regarding God's love, the mood and spirit of the times, as well as the attitude of the prophet. It also fits into the characteristic style and structure of the book. It should be observed here that God always has the proper answer. It is wise for God's prophets to stand in the council of Yahweh and get his message to proclaim and his answers to the complicated questions of life with which they are confronted. In speaking of the preaching of false prophets, the Lord says through Jeremiah:

But if they had stood in my council, then they would have proclaimed my words to my people, and they would have turned them from their evil way, and from the evil of their doings (Jer. 23:22; cf. I Kings 22:19-23; Isa. 6:8-13).

DIVINE LOVE DECLARED IN CONTRASTED DEALINGS WITH JACOB AND ESAU (1:2c-5)

1:2c **"Is not Esau a brother to Jacob?" says Yahweh. "Yet I have loved Jacob;**

3 **Esau I have hated and I have made his mountains a desolation and his property (I gave) to the jackals of the desert."**

4 **Although Edom continually says, "We have been severely beaten, but we shall return and proceed to rebuild the ruins;" thus he says, namely, Yahweh of hosts, "They may build, but I myself shall proceed to tear down; and men shall call them the territory of wickedness, the people whom Yahweh has cursed forever."**

5 **And your eyes will proceed to see and you yourselves**

> will continually say "Let Yahweh be magnified upon
> the border of Israel."

The historical setting pertaining to Esau and Jacob is found in Genesis 25:19-34, and in chapters 27, 28, and 33. Esau was the eldest of the twin sons born to Issac and Rebekah. His name means "hairy one." The younger one came out of the womb of his mother grasping the heel of his brother Esau. He was named Jacob which means "supplanter" or "one who takes by the heel."

As the story of the two brothers unfolds, it is evident that conflict and hatred are determined and that to the end. The birthright appeared early in the picture. Jacob sought it by cheap means at first and then through underhanded deception. Esau was willing to sell it for a bowl of soup, and Rebekah planned to steal it with a young kid prepared as a venison dish. At the same time Isaac was preparing, under a subtle pretext of being on his death bed, to give the prized birthright to Esau.

Back of all of the intrigue and trickery involving the birthright stands God keeping watch over his purpose and design involving the covenant and the blessing. Both Rebekah and Isaac knew something of God's purpose, whether they understood it or not. For before the twins were born, he had declared to Rebekah, "Two nations are in your womb, and two peoples, born of you, shall be divided; the one shall be stronger than the other, the elder shall serve the younger" (cf. Gen. 25:23). It is logical to draw the conclusion that God had seen Jacob as the one with special endowments to be the head of the family and worthy to receive the double portion of the heritage. According to general custom, this was the place of the firstborn. In biblical practice it was given to the one to whom it belonged according to the choice and providence of God. There is no exception to this principle, because it is spiritually conceived and bestowed. Rowley said, "It is ever election for a purpose, and God ever chooses those who are best suited for His purpose."[1] He also said that "election and task were so closely bound together that she (Israel) could not have the one

---

[1]H. H. Rowley, *The Biblical Doctrine of Election* (London: Lutterworth Press, 1964), p. 39.

without the other."[1] In speaking of the office of the prophet, Rowley declared,

And their service is to receive and to communicate the word of God, a word that ever has a revelation of the character and will of God as its essential content.[2]

George Adam Smith has observed:

In the Old Testament predestination is not to character or fate, to salvation or its opposite, to eternal life or eternal punishment, but to service, or some particular form of service, for God and man.[3]

In the immediate context of the Jacob-Esau story, one should conclude that neither of them was worthy to receive the provisions of the birthright and to undertake its covenantal responsibilities. About the only evident distinction between them is that Jacob desired to have it. In assessing Edom, Esau's descendants, it may be declared that they were godless, the incarnation of worldliness and irreligion, and unworthy of the favor of God. Israel, Jacob's offspring, on the other hand, had responded to God's overtures of grace and entered into covenant with him. They had been objects and recipients of his unfailing love. Thus the variation in the character and temperament of the two nations was the deciding factor in their treatment.

The account in Malachi is several hundred years beyond the time of the two erstwhile brothers and is concerned with the progeny of Jacob and Esau. In discussing the heirs of election, Rowley stated:

For the indisputable fact is that Israel has mediated to the world a great spiritual heritage and Edom has not. The character of Jacob is not set forth in very exalted terms, and we know too little of the character of Esau to justify with any confidence the choice of the one rather than the other in terms of character. But if we rightly find in election not the

[1]*Ibid.*, p. 59.

[2]*Ibid.*, p. 111.

[3]George Adam Smith, *Jeremiah* (4th ed.; New York: Harper and Brothers Publishers, 1929), p. 336.

reward of character so much as the summons to service, then the election of Israel and not Edom is justified. For Israel, with all her failures, did through her Remnant render that service, and Edom assuredly did not. There is here, therefore, something deeper than Israelite self-esteem. There is a vindicated faith.[1]

In answer to the request for a clarification of the statement made about God's love, the prophet follows the pattern of his predecessors. Accordingly, he goes back into ancient history and compresses volumes into a few lines. The question he asks, "Is not Esau a brother to Jacob?" is sufficient to heighten their interest to receive the answer, "Yet, I have loved Jacob, but Esau I have hated . . . ." The love of God for Jacob poses no problem, but how is his hatred for Esau to be understood? On the basis of this statement God has been charged with injustice, sinful passion, and partiality. It has been used in support of the doctrine of election to salvation and predestination to reprobation. It should be said here that if election is involved, it is in the light of God's call to service. It is concerned with the accomplishment of his will in the establishment of his kingdom, and the blessing of all mankind through the chosen people. There is no support here or anywhere else in the Bible for predestination to damnation.

The concern for the interpreter in this text is God's hatred of Esau. Because men are sinners they may hate their brothers, even as Jacob and Esau hated each other. But how God, who is altogether righteous and the embodiment of love, can hate anybody or anything but moral evil is the problem. Some of the more evident and serious things with which to wrestle are the language which is used, Hebrew culture and theology, and the Old Testament ethic. One must take note of a restricted understanding of the word hate, the knowledge and purpose of God which are divine and not human, and an effort to completely superimpose the spirit of Christ on Old Testament concepts. Yet another problem, perhaps more serious than any other, is the failure to understand that the Hebrew concept of man and all that concerns him are one and the same. What he

---

[1] Rowley, *The Biblical Doctrine of Election*, p. 71.

thinks, says, does, and possesses can never be regarded separately in an absolute sense. All of these things are man, and man is all of these things.

The Lord hates robbery, wrong, and idolatry (cf. Isa. 61:8; Deut. 12:31). His hatred for Israel is expressed by two faithful prophets (cf. Hos. 9:15; Jer. 12:8). The psalmist proclaims God's hatred for him that loves violence and evil doers (cf. 11:5; 4:4-5). The Lord declares his hatred for Israel's empty, hypocritical worship (cf. Isa. 1:14; Amos 5:21). It was because of the persistent and determined sin of Judah that the Lord declared to Jeremiah "therefore I hate her" (cf. 12:8). The word which is used for hate in Jeremiah is the same word that is found in the text of Malachi.

It has been suggested that the contrasting of the terms love and hate is characteristic in Hebrew logic and Oriental hyperbole. It is simply stated and understood that if God loves Jacob, he hates Esau. There is no middle ground. Although many interpreters do not agree, it is possible that a weaker term than the word hate should be employed. In this sense hate may suggest "love less." The same Hebrew word which is translated "hate" in Malachi 1:3 is rendered "dislike" or "spurn" in other texts (cf. Deut. 21:15; 22:13, 16; 24:3). This same idea is reflected in the translation of Genesis 29:30 which expresses Jacob's attitude toward Rachel and Leah (cf. 1 Sam. 1:4-5). Thus the fortunes of Esau in comparison to Jacob's greater position and blessing are considered to be the result of God's hatred.

History's records provide sufficient explanation and justification of God's wisdom and righteousness in his choices and decisions regarding Jacob and Esau. He sees from the beginning to the end, while man views life in terms of moments (cf. Isa. 29:16; 45:9-10; 55:9). Esau's way of life, freely chosen, invited the judgment of God. Jacob, who chose just as freely, became the recipient of his love and blessing. Edom, Esau's descendants, is pictured as the symbol of hatred, and the type of all people who set themselves against God, inviting his judgment and destruction (cf. Isa. 34:5ff.; 63:1-6; Jer. 49:7-22; Ezek. 25:12-14; Obad. 1-21).

To say that God hates Edom is to reckon with his wrath

against sinners. Theological opinion regarding God's wrath has moved in three basic directions. First, universalism, which assumes everybody ultimately will be saved and delivered from God's wrath, is a popular belief in some circles. Second, annihilation, the cessation of existence or non-being, is believed by others. Third, some feel the eternal judgment of God is visited on impenitent sinners which results in their being separated from God forever (cf. Prov. 29:1; Matt. 25:46).

The anger of Yahweh is perpetual against all whose unwillingness to repent is likewise perpetual. The idea of God's wrath against sin may be revolting, ridiculed, or openly repudiated; but its reality is not changed. It is the other side of the coin whose face is engraved with the word "love." God expresses his anger against sin because of who he is and because of what sin is and does.

Further explanation is given in the words, "and I have made his mountains a desolation, and his property (I gave) to the jackals of the desert." Edom's territory was the rugged mountainous and desert land southeast of the Dead Sea, adjacent to Moab and Judah. This land has been known at various times as Seir, Hor, Edom, and Esau. Part of the economy was derived from farming, but the major source of income came through tolls which were collected from merchants who traversed the caravan route between Syria and Egypt. The Edomites were strong and secure at the time when Israel was liberated from Egypt and was attempting to get to her land. They were involved in conflicts with Israel from time to time, finally being subdued by David and kept in subjection until the time of Ahaz toward the end of the seventh century B.C. Very little is known about this inveterate foe of Israel from this time until her demise as a nation.

It is evidently this time of trouble of the latter years, including the expulsion from her land by the Nabataean Arabs, which is the judgment to which Malachi refers. There is no absolute way of dating this event, but it must have taken place after Nebuchadnezzar's invasions in 586 B.C. It was at this time that it was reported that the Nabataeans had driven the Edomites out of Petra and were in possession of their whole territory in 312 B.C. This event could have occurred in the lifetime of Malachi. A date between 550 and 400 B.C. has been suggested. A visit to Petra, the place that was once a military fortress that was thought to be invincible, is revealing. Forsaken and desolate, it is a grim reminder of the truth of the prophet's words. For Edom's land has been laid waste and has become a habitation of the jackals or wild dogs and other wandering creatures of the desert (cf. Isa. 13:22, 34:13; Jer. 9:11; 10:22; 49:33; 51:37).

The use of the word "continually" (vs. 4) in the translation reflects a possible meaning of the imperfect verb form. The language of the verse is that of the determination and boasting of a proud, self-sufficient, and godless people. They declare that they will rise up out of the ruins of destruction and rebuild. It is possible that these words became a slogan and a rally cry. It is possible that they were part of a popular song which was heard in their streets.

The response of Yahweh to this proud boasting of a nation ground in the dust and humiliated through his judgment is one of calm confidence and determination to act. It is significant that this declaration is made by the use of the term "Yahweh of hosts," which is prominent throughout the book of Malachi, being found at least twenty-four times. Its use here makes it an oath of assurance. The prophets employ this term in such a way as to make it a distinctive peculiar to them. It is sometimes written "Lord Sabaoth." "Sabaoth" is a transliteration of the Hebrew letters into English. This word has been regarded by some who are not conversant with its meaning as a reference to the Sabbath, hence, Lord of the Sabbath. Such is not the meaning of this unique word.

The first use of the term "Lord of hosts" in the Bible is by Hannah in connection with a vow which she made unto the Lord (cf. 1 Sam. 1:11). Its meaning always must be sought in the context where it appears. Sometimes it refers to the angelic hosts; at other times heavenly bodies or starry hosts are intended.Its most prominent use is its reference to the armies of Israel. All three of these meanings appear to be combined on occasion with reference to the armies of Israel. All three of these meanings appear to be combined on occasion with reference to the sovereignty of God and his universal power and

Godhead manifesting itself in all realms of life. This is to suggest that God has all material and spiritual forces at his command (cf. Isa. 40:25-26).

It is on the basis of his sovereign power that God declares his fixed purpose to destroy anything that Edom may start to build. This will be done and exhibited until they earn the title "sin town" or "wicked land." They will be a people upon whose hands or over whose land the inscription will be written, "under God's wrath forever" (cf. Isa. 34:5). This will be Yahweh's just verdict. Its true sense is that they have rebuilt for the last time (cf. Isa. 9:8-12). The declaration is final and irrevocable because Edom's cup of iniquity was overflowing and justice could no longer be withheld.

Psalm 2 is a poetic commentary on this prose account of a nation that has set itself against God. Thus, Edom is put in the world's show window as an exhibition of the folly of fighting against God. The psalm gives support to the fact that sin is a reproach to any people (cf. Prov. 14:34), and that "the wages of sin is death" (cf. Rom. 6:23). Its words appropriately portray God's calm confidence in the face of such rebellion. It speaks of his wrath and pronounces a blessing on all "who take refuge in him."

Verse 5 is a magnificent doxology, an oratorio in a single line. The child's simple prayer begins with the phrase, "God is great." Malachi declares that when the work of God in the visitation of his judgment upon Edom is seen by their very eyes in its full fruition, it will occasion a doxology, ascribing greatness to Yahweh upon the border of Israel.

Some translations have "beyond the border of Israel" (ASV, RSV). This would make the results of God's work apply to people and things outside of the confines of Israel. In this case, it would involve the people of Edom. This is hardly the meaning in this context. The translation "above" or "upon the border of Israel" is more natural as is evidenced in its usage in numerous other Old Testament texts (Gen. 1:7; 27:12; Ex. 5:21; Num. 9:17; Deut. 26:19; 2 Kings 25:28; Neh. 9:19). The prophet is magnifying the fact of Yahweh's love and protection as a canopy over Israel. At the same time he visits Edom with the blast of his judgment and destruction. This is in answer to the question which was raised about his love in the key word "wherein?"

George L. Robinson, in his summary of Malachi 1:2-5, said: The prophet shows that Jehovah still loves Israel, because Israel's lot stands in such marked contrast to Edom's. Israel, though exiled, has been brought back from captivity; Edom has been permanently driven out of its mountain stronghold, and will never return—being irretrievably and inexorably banished. [1]

<hr>

[1]Robinson, *The Twelve Minor Prophets*, p. 163.

III. Divine Love Dishonored

This portion of Malachi, extending from 1:6 through 2:9, is concerned with the sins of the priesthood. The whole nation's welfare is involved, however, because the priests are the leaders in worship and religious instruction.

THE FACT OF DISHONORED LOVE (1:6a)

1:6a "A son repeatedly honors his father, and a servant (fears) his master; now if a father am I, where is my honor?" Yahweh of hosts says to you, the priests who despise my name.

The fact of dishonored love is declared in the analogy of the son and servant relationship to the father and master. The language suggests that it is the customary thing for a son to honor his father and for a servant to fear his master. Yahweh is declared and magnified as father throughout Israel's history (cf. Ex. 4:22; Deut. 32:6; Isa. 43:6; 63:16; 103:13). He is father by creation, redemption, and providential care. These words magnify relationship and responsibility. They are given in a context that requires no explanation. The Semitic people, because of their dominant patriarchal culture, were characterized by parental respect. Honor was both expected by and given to a father. This simply expressed the norm that prevailed. The words of the text are not concerned with infractions and deviations pertaining to parental respect. This fact is evidenced and magnified both in the precepts of their law codes and in the privacy of family relationships (cf. Ex. 20:12; Lev. 19:3; Matt. 15:14; Eph. 6:2). Although love is expressed, authority is the dominant emphasis in the word father.

The words honor and glory are closely related in Hebrew, both of them coming from the same root form. Either word gives the same basic idea. To honor is to glorify, to exalt or to make great. One who honors another glorifies or ascribes glory to him. Likewise, one who glorifies another honors him.

The concept of Israel as Yahweh's servant is one of long standing (cf. Ex. 3:12; 9:1; I Sam. 3:9; 1 Kings 8:66). It is customary for a servant to fear his master. "Fears," inserted in the text, is found in the next phrase. It also is given in the Septuagint, the Greek translation of the Old Testament (also call "LXX"). The servant-master relationship was thoroughly understood in Malachi's time. It was a vital part of the culture of that day. Individuals in the nation were servants, but the nation itself was the servant of a foreign master.

The prophet continues as he addresses the priests who despise Yahweh's name. The charge is made that the priests withheld from Yahweh the filial honor which is due to him as a father, and the humble fear which he can claim as a master is not given. The indictment is both serious and sad. It comes from the Lord. It is directed to the priests, an important and significant segment of the nation's spiritual leadership. The word "priest" in this study should be given the meaning of "minister" in the sense that one who serves the Lord as a leader in worship and spiritual instruction, ministers unto him

and his people. If such disrespect and disobedience characterized the way of their spiritual leadership, what can be expected
of the average citizen? Yahweh was being despised when honor
and faithful service were his due as a father and a master. The
faltering, failing priests had been challenged and condemned
previously. Hosea charged them with trapping, robbing, and
murdering the people (cf. 5:1; 6:9). Micah accused them of
performing their work for financial returns (cf. 3:11).

To despise is to regard with contempt. It may be depicted by
the lifting of the head loftily and disdainfully in self-sufficient
pride. It is to repudiate a thing as worthless. Esau despised the
birthright (cf. Gen. 25:34). Malachi declares that the priests are
despising the name or person of God. His name, like his
holiness, means his sole Godhead or Deity. Warning is given
against taking his name in vain or using it lightly (cf. Ex.
20:7). It is for the sake of his name that he withholds or
restrains his anger (cf. Isa. 48:9-11). This is emphasized
throughout the book of Malachi (see Introduction). The attitude
of the people is one of contempt toward God himself. This
attitude was outwardly expressed through the conduct of the
designated ministers who were called of God. Their sin is in
offering polluted offerings upon his altar.

The people of Israel declared that Yahweh was their father
and master, but they were not willing to submit to the demands
which such a relationship entailed. This illustrates the democ-
racy of privilege and the defaulting of responsibility. It is the
pursuit of peace while desiring the spoils of war. It is a
thirsting after righteousness while pursuing after sinful passions and worldly lusts. It is the desire to have a free church in
a free state with no responsibility of service or support. It is the
spirit of uninvolvement and irresponsibility. It is the travesty
of learning without study, morals without morality, wages
without work, and religion without righteousness.

THE DENIAL OF DISHONORED LOVE (1:6b)

1:6b But you say, "Wherein have we despised your name?"
Again, a bill of particulars is requested by the use of the

characteristic "wherein?" This marks the haughty spirit of the people as they talk back to God and his prophet. They are becoming more adamant and determined in their sin.

THE MEANS BY WHICH DIVINE LOVE IS DISHONORED (1:7-8)

1:7 By keeping on offering upon my altar bread being polluted. But you say, "Wherein have we polluted you?" In your saying the table of Yahweh is contemptible.

8 And when you repeatedly offer blind cattle for a sacrifice, it is no evil? And when you continue to offer crippled and sick *animals,* **it is no evil? Present it now to your governor; will he be pleased with you? Or will he proceed to lift up your face? (show you favor or accept your person?) says Yahweh of hosts.**

Worship in Israel involved the offering of animals as well as the products of the field upon the altar. The words "altar" and "table" appear to be used interchangeably. The altar stood in the outer court in front of the temple. The offerings which were brought were the means of renewing and strengthening covenant relationships. Burnt offerings symbolized the complete dedication of the worshipper. They were regarded as having been consumed by the Lord as evidence that the offerer was both surrendered to him and accepted by him. The worship which was being offered and which Malachi condemns was the very opposite of that which is described here. The covenant was ignored, and God was dishonored both by the worshipper and his worship.

It is to be noted by the use of participles that the offense with which the people are charged is the continuous practice of offering polluted bread upon the altar. It was not something which was done in an unguarded moment. It was a determined way of life. The terms bread, food, and meat are expressive of one and the same thing. They were either animal or vegetable offerings. The language and setting suggest a banquet in which the Lord and the worshipper share in a spiritual feast. Polluted bread may be that which was made with rotten grain, or bread that was molded. If it were an animal, it was blemished in some way and not fit to eat or to offer as a gift (cf. Lev. 3:11, 16; 21:6ff.; 22:25; Num. 28:2, 24). Thus the Lord was invited to participate in a polluted banquet.

The request for clarification of the means by which Yahweh was being polluted is answered by the prophet. Not only were the offerings substandard, but also the attitudes and thoughts regarding the altar were contemptible. Both these things go together. Actions spring from attitudes. An indifferent and despicable attitude toward acceptable ritual in worship is abhorred because it reveals a low spiritual vitality and unconcern for God and his claims. What one does is the outward manifestation of what he is in his inner being (cf. Deut. 5:29; Prov. 23:7; Matt. 15:17-20). The worship which was offered was unacceptable, because the offerings did not meet divine specifications, and the way which the people lived was unacceptable (cf. Micah 6:6-8). Thus the displeasure of the Lord is expressed because of this twofold sin. Either one of these sins makes worship unacceptable.

The same kind of irreverence and indifference is too much a part of our worship and service. The minister too often offers an inferior sermon on the altar to his congregation because of his failure to pray and study. The service which he renders during the week may be poorly done because of his inferior spirit. In his chapter on Hosea, Raymond Calkins said:

> Irreligion is at the root of all our troubles today as truly as it was in the days of Hosea. And in order to reinstate religion it is necessary to have an intelligent, a competent, a courageous and devoted ministry. This perhaps is the greatest need of the Church today.[1]

The worship of the man in the pew may be characterized in the same way. That which he offers as service during the week may be marked by a spiritual inferiority complex and an attitude of indifference.

The prophet continues his condemnation of unacceptable worship in verse 8. The animals which the people offered to the Lord were worthless. They could not be eaten, sold, or given as

---

[1] Raymond Calkins, *The Modern Message of the Minor Prophets* (New York: Harper and Brothers, 1947), p. 47.

gifts. This reveals contempt for God and worship, because an offering that costs the giver nothing in reality is not an offering at all (cf. 2 Sam. 24:24-25). The questions which are asked about these offerings indicate both the sarcasm of the prophet and the contempt of the people. In order to magnify the offense of which they were guilty, the prophet, in a sense, said "If it is no evil, offer these blind, crippled, and sick animals to your governor." It is possible that animals were given to the governor to pay taxes, or a fine; they may have been presented as a bribe, or as a means of expressing friendship and seeking some favor. Apparently, the latter is the meaning here. The prophet then asks if the governor will be pleased with them or show them the favor which they hoped to obtain through their gifts. The question implies a negative answer. It also reveals that they had a higher regard for the governor and his office than they had for God. When there is no respect for God, worship has no worth.

So in this generation some would offer as gifts to God their old bills which they cannot collect. Charity is rendered to the needy in order to avoid criticism from those who are able to pay, or as an effort to salve an otherwise accusing conscience. Time and service are given to curry favor with the public. Are such offerings characterized in the so-called deathbed repentance of one who has lived his whole life apart from God, yet with the knowledge of God and in the atmosphere and influence of the Christian religion? When he comes to die, he blows the smoke of the flickering candle of a burned out and dissipated life into the face and nostrils of God. He desires that this shall be an acceptable offering. Such conduct is as offensive to God as that for which Israel was sharply condemned. It is a repudiation of God, an insult to his high and holy character, and is rejected as unworthy and unacceptable.

One can hardly refute the argument that much of the scorn which is heaped upon the church today by one who professes no religious faith is because he sees much profession and too little practice among the churchmen with whom he associates. A down-to-earth garden variety of the flowers of honesty, purity, kindness, forgiveness, brotherly love, and godliness must grace our tables of regeneration, justification, and sanctification if beauty and fragrance are to be provided for a sordid world. If there are goods in the warehouse, they must be displayed in the show window. This will dry up the cesspools of cynicism, bitterness, and hatred which continue to send forth a foul odor and a constant stream of vituperations against the church and the Christian cause (cf. Eccl. 10:1).

One may sit in his doctrinal castles and criticize all who do not say "shibboleth" with him. It is possible to magnify the sins of racism, lying, and cheating, and hurl vilifying word bombs at the intellectual atheists. At the same time, one may ignore the people of other races, practice deception and dishonesty, and bask in the sunshine of his practical atheism, living as if God does not exist.

THE RESULTS OF DISHONORED LOVE (1:9-14)

God's Favor is Withdrawn (1:9)

1:9 And now, I pray you, entreat the favor of God, that he may proceed to be gracious unto us; from your hand is this; will he show favor to any of you? says Yahweh of hosts.

The Lord is said to be waiting to be gracious and to show mercy as a God of justice (cf. Ex. 34:6, 7; Isa. 30:18). He is gracious and compassionate because he keeps his covenant (cf. 2 Kings 13:23). The prophets declare that God's gracious acts are withheld because of sin (cf. Amos 5:14-15; Isa. 27:11). Man's entreaty to the Lord for his gracious help bears witness to his need and the belief that God can and will meet his needs (cf. Pss. 6:1; 9:13; 25:16; 31:10). Man is to show favor and be gracious to his fellow man, because God deals graciously with him (cf. Gen. 33:11). A part of the minister's responsibility is to entreat God to be gracious unto his people as he offers the benediction (cf. Num. 6:24-26).

In the face of these significant facts, the prophet mocks and ridicules with tantalizing irony. He says in effect, "You have brought offerings to Yahweh that you would be ashamed to give to your governor. You know you would not find favor with him. Now I dare you to beseech God's favor and obtain all of his gracious blessings for us. This surely is within the scope of your duty and you have the power to bring it to pass." Some interpreters suggest that the prophet was telling the priests that since they had brought the people into disfavor with God, it was their responsibility to effect the necessary reconciliation. He then asks, "Will he be gracious toward us? Will he accept any of your persons or lift up your faces?" The idea here is, "Will he show you any favor?" Obviously, the question expects a negative answer and may be rendered, "He surely will not."

Isaiah declares:

Behold, the Lord's hand is not shortened, that it cannot save,
or his ear dull, that it cannot hear;
but your iniquities have made a separation
between you and your God, and your sins have
hid his face from you so that he does not hear.
For your hands are defiled with blood and your
fingers with iniquity; your lips have spoken
lies, your tongue mutters wickedness. (Isaiah 59:1-3).

Makes Worship at the Temple
Unacceptable (1:10)

1:10 Oh, that there were one among you that would shut the doors, that you would not *ever* cause my altar to burn in vain! There is not for me any pleasure in you says Yahweh of hosts, and an offering I shall never accept from your hand.

The King James Version inserts the words "for nought." This is to indicate that no one would perform the service of shutting the doors of the temple or build a fire on the altar without being paid for it. The words "for nought" are not in the text. The idea which such a translation suggests obscures the meaning which is intended.

This verse is a continuation of the theme of verses 7 and 8. That which was taking place at the house of God in the name of worship was offensive and worthless in the eyes of God. He expressed a deep longing for someone to close the doors which gave access to the temple. Although the word "temple" is not in the text, we are correct in concluding that such is the meaning. It does call attention to burning (fire is assumed) on the altar which stood in front of the temple. Thus the concern expressed is that the empty, unacceptable kind of worship would be discontinued.

In order to understand the gravity of such action, if it had been carried out, it is necessary to consider the meaning of the temple and its place in the worship life and experiences of the people. The desire to erect the temple evidently was first conceived by David. He considered it to be a more suitable place for God's abode than a tent (cf. 2 Sam. 7:1ff.). This dream which David was not permitted to carry out was accomplished by Solomon (cf. 1 Kings 6:1ff.; 7:51). When the temple was destroyed by Nebuchadnezzar's armies in 586 B.C., it was regarded as the most tragic thing that had befallen the people of Israel. To close the temple would symbolize the withdrawal of the Lord's presence and blessing (cf. 1 Sam. 4:21-22; 1 Kings 8:27-30). The nation would lose one of its strongest unifying influences, and the people would be denied the privilege of some of their greatest spiritual experiences (1 Sam. 3:1ff.; Isa. 6:1-8).

These solemn words in verse 10 express keen disappointment on the one hand and a serious indictment on the other. The disappointment is felt because of what such worship expressed regarding the attitude of the people toward God. As a father, he longed to have the sincere expressions of love and praise which he deserved from his children. The indictment is not only a repudiation of the worship but of the people who offered it. Outward forms utilized in worship, if they are to mean anything to God or man, must be the expression of penitent hearts of people who desire to be reconciled to God and to have his blessing. When one is spiritually dead, the worship which he offers in outward and formal ritual is dead also. Unacceptable sacrifices, cynicism toward worship, immorality and corruption are born of unbelief and ingratitude. People who believe in God and love him cannot go on practicing sin.

The prophets did not condemn the sacrificial system, but

they did condemn the manner in which it was sometimes observed. According to the laws governing the sacrificial system of the Old Testament, an acceptable offering was expressive of the recognition of broken fellowship, penitence, and devotion to the covenant relationship (cf. Lev. 5:5; 16:21; Num. 5:6). The distinction in the offerings of Cain and Abel was neither in the quality nor in the quantity of what they offered, but in their spirit and attitude as they came before God. The prophets preceding Malachi speak sharply against worship which is not in accord with the above principles of acceptable worship. Samuel asks, "Has the Lord as great delight in burnt offerings and sacrifices, as in obeying the voice of the Lord?" He then admonished, "Behold, to obey is better than sacrifice, and to harken than the fat of rams" (cf. 1 Sam. 15:22). Hosea's words, "For I desire steadfast love and not sacrifice, the knowledge of God, rather than burnt offerings," speak to the matter (cf. Hosea 6:6). To a people who expressed willingness to give anything that God required even if it meant sacrificing their children, Micah proclaims, "He has showed you, O man, what is good; and what does the Lord require of you but to do justice, and to love kindness, and to walk humbly with your God?" (cf. Micah 6:8). Contemporaries of Hosea and Micah express the same deep concern (cf. Amos 5:21-24; Isa. 1:11-15; cf. Psa. 51:17; Prov. 21:3).

Thus God's repudiation of the offerings and of those who officiated at the altar was not a new thing. The examples of Nadab and Abihu, Aaron's sons, and Hophni and Phinehas, son of Eli, are to be remembered (cf. Lev. 10:1ff.; 1 Sam. 2:12ff.). Let all who minister at the altar and in all holy things be warned of sloven, cheap, unacceptable service, and impurity of life. Worship that is not offered in true devotion to God is a hypocritical farce. Scott has put it in these forceful words:

> Hence the formal worship which takes no account of Yahweh's real nature and which does not stir the depths of life, is rejected by God, not with indifferent disdain, but with the loathing of one whose being is outraged.[1]

[1]R. B. Y. Scott, *The Relevance of the Prophets*, p. 108.

God is Turning to Others Who
Honor Him (1:11)

1:11 "For from the rising of the sun even unto its going down great is my name among the heathen; and in every place incense is being offered to my name, and a pure offering, because great is my name among the heathen," says Yahweh of hosts.

Several interpretations have been considered in seeking to understand the meaning of this verse. It must be said here that none of these interpretations is without its problems.

"From the rising of the sun even unto its going down" suggests that the whole range of human dwelling, wherever people may be found, is being considered. It is evident that God's name is great among heathen people where incense, a symbol of prayer, is being considered. It is evident that God's name is great among heathen people where incense, a symbol of prayer, is being offered to God's name. This is accompanied by a pure offering, in contrast to the lame, blind, and sick animals which the Jews were offering. The word used here for offering suggests a gift of any kind which is given in worship as a tribute to God. The conclusion is that God's name is great or magnified among the heathen. This fact is stated twice in the verse for emphasis. It should be observed further that the incense and offering used in worship are being offered to *God's name.* These things are being emphasized because they constitute both the problem and the challenge of the text.

Some consider this verse to be descriptive of the worship of Yahweh by dispersed Jews who were scattered over a wide area of the world, including Babylon, Persia, Egypt, and other places. Information regarding the fact of such worship has been made available and serves to substantiate this claim. It is reasonable to believe that Malachi would have had some knowledge of these people and their worship. It is a valid conclusion that he would have considered their worship, even under more limited and difficult circumstances, to be offered with a greater degree of reverence and sincerity than that which was being offered in Jerusalem by the Jews at the temple where

God was thought to be dwelling.[1] Such an interpretation has significance because of a Jewish belief that God could be worshipped in an acceptable manner only in Palestine. This interpretation would suffice for an explanation of that which was going on among the heathen or in heathen lands, but making it apply to the Diaspora is perhaps a forced meaning, more eisegesis than exegesis. The entire emphasis is on the heathen and his worship. Nothing is said about the Jews, scattered abroad or otherwise. There is a problem also concerning the widespread area involving the whole range of heathen habitation. It does not appear that the Jews were that widely scattered.

The KJV and the ASV translate the verbs in the future, making the text read "my name 'shall be great,'" and "a pure offering 'shall be offered.'" This makes it possible to apply the meaning to the New Testament era, looking to the time when the gospel would be preached and greater missionary endeavor would be exerted by the church in evangelizing heathen nations. Gentiles would see the light and would come to the Lord in great force, offering themselves as living sacrifices and a sweet smelling savour in gratitude for his saving grace. This is a great truth, and it is coming to pass in many places. But the question may be asked as to how this transaction taking place hundreds of years later would meet the need and purpose of Malachi's time. This would be irrelevant and without force.

If verse eleven is translated correctly from the Hebrew text, the verbs must be put in the present tense. This means that it is not to be read "my name shall be great," but "my name is great among the heathen." This translation is supported by the fact that the verb "shall be" is put in italics in the KJV and the ASV to indicate that it is not in the original Hebrew text. Therefore, the present tense is followed in this study, because it is supported by syntax, grammar, and the context. This is

[1]J. M. P. Smith, W. H. Ward, and Julius A. Bewer, *A Critical and Exegetical Commentary on the Book of Malachi.* The International Critical Commentary, ed. by Samuel Rolles Driver, Alfred Plummer, and Charles Augustus Briggs (Edinburgh: T. & T. Clark, 1912), pp. 30-33.

something which Malachi sees taking place in his time. It is going on while he is speaking.

In the light of this translation the prophet might be saying that the sincere worship of heathen gods was acceptable to the one true God. Some regard the emphasis of the prophet to be on motivation rather than on the act of worship. Matthews has pointed out that Malachi was a monotheist who considered motives to be more significant than outward acts. The importance of motive over against form is considered to be of ancient vintage (cf. Ex. 20:13-14; Lev. 4:2, 13, 14).[1] Matthews further observed:

> . . . he (Malachi) was ready to acknowledge that heathen who were sincere in their worship were more acceptable to Yahweh than the Jew who with greater light was indifferent to his heritage seems to be the point of the verse.[2]

Bennett has expressed a similar view with the clarification that the prophet was not praising the heathen in his worship but shaming the leaders of his nation in seeking to bring them to a greater devotion to God. The emphasis is on the reverence of the heathen who had limited knowledge, toward God, and the contempt expressed toward God by the Jew.[3]

Eli Cashdan quoted Hertz who said:

> The implication seems to be that offerings brought by heathens to their gods are in reality intended for God. This view is supported by the statement in the Talmud that even the idolators call him "the God of gods." "Even the heathen nations that worship the heavenly hosts pay tribute to a Supreme Being, and in this way honour my name; and the offerings which they present (indirectly) unto me are animated by a pure spirit, God looking to the heart of the worshipper."[4]

---

[1] I. G. Matthews, "Haggai, Malachi," *An American Commentary on the Old Testament* (Philadelphia: The Judson Press, 1935), p. 19.

[2] *Ibid.*

[3] Bennett, "Malachi," p. 378.

[4] Cashdan, "Malachi," p. 340.

Dentan regards this as Malachi's

> . . . magnificent and unparalleled assertion that all true
> worship, even though that of the heathen who think they are
> worshipping other gods, is really offered to Yahweh, who is
> the God not only of Israel but of all the earth.[1]

An effort to understand the above conclusions reveals that
sincere heathen worship provides both a marked contrast to and
a condemnation of the hypocritical worship which was being
offered to Yahweh by the Jews. The limited knowledge of the
heathen is set over against the advantage of the heritage,
knowledge, and training of the Jews. This is considered to be
the means used by the prophet to shame his people and to
awaken them to greater devotion and responsibility. It is
further claimed that all true worship of the heathen is really
offered to Yahweh in spite of the fact that the heathen thinks
he is worshipping other gods.

These interpretations do not say that sincerity is sufficient
and may be considered as a substitute for the knowledge of
God. Nothing is said about the salvation of the heathen, nor
that his ignorant worship of God will bring him to a forgiving,
saving experience with God. This evidently is considered to be
something for God to determine by his wisdom and to make
possible by his providence. The responsibility for Christian
missions is neither declared nor denied.

It should be observed that if Malachi intended to convey the
meaning which is given above, no other Scripture has been cited
in support of this claim. That heathen worship is accepted and
praised as if it were the worship of God and the magnifying of
his name has no support anywhere in the Bible. Such an idea is
inadmissible and unacceptable. The Scriptures provide little
help on the worship which is offered unto idols and heathen
gods, but they do not imply that such worship may in any way
be the worship of the one true God. On the other hand,
numerous passages can be cited as evidence that the Lord is
not pleased with idolatry and heathen worship (cf. Deut.
6:10-15; 7:1ff.; 32:17; Isa. 44:9-23; 1 Cor. 10:20). In the light of
these facts, it may be asked why heathen worship would be

---

[1] Dentan, "The Book of Malachi," p. 1120.

approved by Malachi even if it is only intended to magnify sincerity as a means of shaming his people for their hypocrisy. It seems that the prophet's emphasis on the correct ritual (cf. 3:2b-4), his condemnation of the heathen practice of sorcery (cf. 3:5), and of marriages to foreign women (cf. 2:11) are strong evidences to the contrary.

Another interpretation has been offered by others but generally is rejected as untenable without any effort to explore its meaning or merits. It is suggested that the intention of Malachi appears to be that the sincere worship of God-fearing people in heathen lands who had turned from their idols is both pleasing to the Lord and a condemnation of the worship which was being offered by the cynical, hypocritical Jews. Francisco has observed:

> There are no verbs in the Hebrew of this verse. This may be a prediction, but usually such a construction demands a verb. If the present time is intended, as the context suggests, the verse means that Gentiles throughout the world (perhaps proselytes) are offering more acceptable worship to the one God than unfaithful Judah. [1]

An attempt will be made to deal with the emphasis on the name of God which is paramount in the text. To speak of the name of one is to speak of the person himself. It is an emphasis on his character. The text declares that God's name is magnified, and the worship which is offered is in his name. Thus the heathen are said to be worshipping *the God* and not *their Gods.* It is further observed that the one who speaks of this worship and is being magnified by it is Yahweh of hosts (cf. 1:10-11). It is to be admitted that heathen worship may be regarded as a reaching out after God, but the text here goes beyond that.

The major difficulty in this interpretation is the fact that the name of Yahweh is declared to be great from the rising to the setting of the sun, and incense and a pure offering are being offered to him in every place. To take this to mean that the whole heathen world was bowing to Yahweh would be incredi-

---

[1] Clyde T. Francisco, *Introducing the Old Testament* (Nashville: Broadman Press, 1950), p. 183.

ble. It has no support in biblical or contemporary history of that time. It should not be necessary, however, to count great numbers of Yahweh worshippers to validate Malachi's claim. Only a remnant of heathen worshippers converted to Yahweh who were scattered among the nations would suffice. It is possible that many believed in God while others remained in the darkness of their unbelief without excuse (cf. Rom. 1:18-20). Speaking of man's knowledge of God, Davidson declared:

... He may be known from nature; i.e., not only that we may see God there whom we already know, but that we may discover God there though formerly unknown.[1]

If supporting evidence is necessary, let it be remembered that Abraham was converted from dense paganism, perhaps the worship of "Sin," the moon god, in Ur of the Chaldees. He brought his knowledge of Yahweh God with him when he came to Canaan several centuries before the time of Malachi (cf. Acts 7:1; Gen. 12:1-7). Melchizedek, who was already in Canaan, also was a worshipper of Abraham's God (cf. Gen. 14:18-22). Jethro, the father-in-law- of Moses, worshipped God, apparently having knowledge of Yahweh, before Moses joined him in the wilderness of Sinai (cf. Ex. 3:1; 18:1ff.). It should not seem strange to believe that a goodly number of people in heathen lands had come to know the Lord by the time of Malachi in the fifth century B.C. The Hebrew law regarding the reception of proselytes to the faith is clear (cf. Lev. 24:22).

This interpretation magnifies the purpose of God involving the blessing of all people (Gen. 12:1-3). It also considers and magnifies the effective witness for several centuries of faithful Jews to the Lord among the heathen. The prophets, including Jonah, preached to the heathen from time to time. It is true that their preaching often emphasized the judgment of the Lord, but such preaching can have good effects. The Diaspora referred to above may have contributed to this witness. Rowley said:

It is probable that the great majority of the proselytes were men and women who continued in their own land, and who

---

[1]A. B. Davidson, *The Theology of the Old Testament*, ed. by S. D. F. Salmond (Edinburgh: T. and T. Clark, 1904), p. 79.

were so impressed with the quality of life of the Jews of the Dispersion that they sought to know and share something of their religious life. [1]
The period of the Babylonian captivity provided the Jews their finest hour, and biblical records reveal that the more faithful ones took full advantage of the opportunity. Heathen people were continually traversing Palestine and even living there from time to time. There are evidences of their becoming proselytes to the Hebrew faith (cf. Josh. 6:25; Heb. 11:31; Ruth 1:16-17; 2 Kings 5:17; Isa. 65:1; Rom. 10:20-21).

It is obvious that the theology of this verse is in the spirit of the New Testament and is the forerunner of that which Jesus and the Apostle Paul enunciated (cf. Jno. 4:19-24; Acts 17:22-28; Rom. 1:18ff.). It declares that God is not a localized deity whose power and Godhead are known and praised only by Israel. It is proof that God cannot be imprisoned in a cubicle of narrow Hebrew nationalism and that the word of God is not bound (cf. 2 Tim. 2:9).

Malachi sees the drawing of a new day and a light in a dark night in the sincere worship which is being offered unto Yahweh in heathen lands. Such worship anticipates the coming of the universal kingdom of God which is envisioned by Malachi's predecessors (cf. Isa. 56:1-8; 66:18-21; Zech. 2:11; Micah 4:1-5; Hab. 2:14). That Yahweh may be worshipped in heathen lands magnifies the love and power of God. God's name is made great among the heathen through his works by which he brings them to reverence him (cf. Ex. 15:11-16; Zeph. 2:11; Ps. 46:9-11). There is an emphasis on the responsibility of Israel to bless all the families of the earth (cf. Gen. 12:1-3), and an encouragement to the heathen to enter the door of hope which is open to them (cf. Isa. 45:22). Here lies the basis of the concept of spiritual Israel, composed of Gentiles as well as Jews. Warning is given to the people of national Israel that they must be of the remnant of this true spiritual Israel if they are to continue in the favor of Yahweh and to fulfill his purpose as a fruitful vine (cf. Isa. 51-10). This thought anticipates the New Testament era and the proclamation of the gospel to all who never have heard (cf. Matt. 28:18-20; Rom. 10:13-17).

[1] Rowley, *The Biblical Doctrine of Election*, p. 89.

*God's Name is Profaned and the Way
of the People is Cursed (1:12-14)*

**1:12 But you are keeping on profaning it, in your saying, the
table of the Lord is polluted and its fruit, being despised
is its food.**

This verse is a transition and a contrast of verse 11. There is
worship among heathen people by which the name of Yahweh is
being magnified, while the people in Israel are profaning
continuously that name and complaining about worship and its
requirements. Their offense is emphasized further by the fact
that the Hebrews by covenant, trust, training, and world
mission were obligated to reverence and to make great the name
or person of Yahweh (cf. Ex. 19:4-6; Deut. 6:4-9).

The charge indicates that the people are delinquent in their
spiritual life, detestable in attitudes, and degenerate in religious
performance. They considered the altar to be unholy, and they
despised the meaning and significance of the worship. A study
of the larger context of Malachi will provide additional help in
interpreting this verse (cf. 1:8, 12; 2:1-3).

**1:13 Also you say, Behold, what a weariness, and you have
caused snorting at him, says Yahweh of hosts, and you
bring that which was taken by violence, also the lame,
and the sick, thus you bring the offering; should I
accept it from your hand? says Yahweh.**

This is a continuation and enlargement of the thought which
is expressed in verse 12. To be weary is not to be taken to mean
that the people had worn themselves out serving and worshipping the Lord. Its meaning is that the service of the Lord was
unsavory, vexatious, irksome, and generally a hardship. They
were tired and worn out with all of this business of going to
church, singing, praying, and making offerings. The term snort
suggests anger, exhausted patience, and a readiness to fight. It
is the picture of a ferocious animal that is ready to spring on its
victim. The translation reflects the causative aspect of the verb.
This indicates that the snorting was being caused by those who
officiated in worship and was being done by the people in
general. It is an outgrowth of the distorted philosophy and the
spiritual bankruptcy of the priests. It is expressive of a

contemptible attitude toward worship and ultimately toward God whom they profess to love and to desire to serve. Both worship and God himself are valued for a cheap price on the market of appreciation.

The personal pronoun "him" is rendered by some translations as "it." It should be observed that the Hebrew language has no neuter gender. It is advisable at times to render a pronoun as a neuter, because the context would be better served by it. Some interpreters seem to think that the use of "it" is an attempt to soften and make less harsh the attitude which characterizes the spirit of the people. They are said to snort at the offerings and the requirements of worship in general. When consideration is given to the fact that the worship is directed to the Lord, the translation "him" seems to be the right choice.

The offerings which the worshippers brought served to magnify their wrong spirit and contemptible attitude toward Yahweh. That which was taken by violence is considered to be some animal that was either stolen or snatched away from the jaws of a wild beast as salvage. The latter would seem to be the sense here. All of the offerings which they were bringing were rejected as unworthy of him whom they worshipped and a violation of the specified requirements.

The Lord's repudiation of such worship and service is seen in the question which is directed to them. "Should I accept it (the offering) from your hand?" The answer expected is a negative one. There was no need to argue the point. It was readily obvious to them that the gifts were unacceptable (cf. 1:8). It should be observed here that the LXX adds "of hosts" to the word Yahweh. This rendering is in keeping with Malachi's usage of the phrase throughout the book.

> **1:14 Now going on being cursed is the one who keeps on deceiving, when there is in his flock a male, and he keeps on vowing and sacrificing a spoiled thing to the Lord; for a great king am I, says Yahweh of hosts, and my name is going on being reverenced among the heathen.**

This verse is marked by its use of participles which reveal both the continuous character and the permanence of what is taking place. This is applicable both to the practice of the people and the judgment or the curse of Yahweh upon them.

The sin which is described here has to do with deception and failure to keep a promised vow. Vows frequently were made to the Lord in a time of crisis. Israel's history is replete with such examples (cf. Gen. 28:20; 31:13; 1 Sam. 1:11; 2 Sam. 15:7; Jonah 1:16; Ps. 16:13; 116:18). Sometimes vows were made as a means of seeking God's favor. At other times they were meant to be an expression of thanksgiving for blessings which had been received. Occasionally, they were pledged with the hope of averting or stopping some judgment.

It is not known just why the vow was made which is alluded to here. It is clear that a specific offering of a male animal is pledged in connection with the vow. After some days when the pressure was off or the blessing had been received, it was time to pay the vow. At this point the mind of the worshipper was changed. His love and appreciation became cold and he judged that his vow either was too much or that he could get by with something less than he had purposed to do. After all God was far away, the vow was voluntary, and no one knew what he had vowed. He, therefore, paid the vow with a corrupt or blemished animal which he considered to be less costly and at the same time sufficient. The sin reveals a defective character and a defaulting in life's highest and most sacred obligation. It is judged to be basic dishonesty and hypocritical mockery. It is further magnified by the fact that the sin is against God who is a great king and is so recognized by the heathen who stand in awe before him.

The kingship of Yahweh over Israel is expressed in numerous ways in the Old Testament. He is sovereign over his people by divine choice and he is the one who protects and delivers in times of distress (cf. Num. 23:21; Deut. 33:5). His rule is declared to be everlasting, and it prevails over the whole world (cf. Ex. 15:17-18; Isa. 33:21-22; 43:14-15; Jer. 10:7-10). The ark of the covenant has been regarded by interpreters as the throne of God. This indicates that the kingship of Yahweh is of ancient vintage (cf. Ex. 15:18; 19:5ff.; Deut. 33:5; Judg. 8:23; 1 Sam. 8:7; Isa. 6:5). The Psalms refer to God as king in numerous places and with significant glorifying terms. He is said to be king over the whole earth, clothed with majesty, and the one by whom the sons of Zion are to triumph (cf. Pss. 47:7; 93:1; 149:2). Isaiah portrays God as the king of Israel and as king on Mount Zion (cf. 44:6; 24:23). It is a sad indictment and a revelation of human depravity when the love of God is least acknowledged at the point of its greatest manifestations.

A man like David may rise up and cast aside his kingly robes and declare that such a criminal is worthy of death before he perceives the import of the deed. One needs to consider *his* vows or perhaps what vows *he* should make before he offers his condemnation of another. It is possible for God to be given the remnants of time, talents, affections, service, and possessions instead of that which is his due. A serious warning is sounded in the face of long profession and short practice. The Saviour declares, "Not every one who says to me, 'Lord, Lord,' shall enter the kingdom of heaven" (Matt. 7:21). Salvation is not by works, but its purpose and proof are seen in works (Eph. 2:8-10).

IV. Divine Love Threatens Punishment

This aspect of divine love magnifies the longsuffering nature of God. An urgent appeal is made to reason that seeks to produce repentance and to avert the visitation of further judgment. It is marked by the entreaty and plaintive plea of Yahweh through another prophet when he says:

Come now and let us reason together, says Yahweh; though your sins be as scarlet, they may be as white as snow; though they be red like crimson, they may be as wool. If you be willing and obedient, you shall eat of the good of the land; but if you rebel, you shall be devoured with the sword; for the mouth of Yahweh has spoken. (Isaiah 1:18-20)[1]

The use of the verb "may be" gives the sense of the subjective mood, indicating that a thing is possible. The forgiveness of sin is declared to be possible, if there are willingness and obedience on the part of the people. If rebellion is pursued, judgment is inevitable. The experiences of other

[1] The author's translation.

prophets and the recipients of divine forgiveness give added support to this fundamental fact (cf. 2 Sam. 12:7ff.; Joel 2:18-20: Jonah 3:5-10; Amos 7:1-6). Likewise, the rebellious and impenitent have experienced the inevitable judgment of God who does not withhold his wrath forever (cf. 1 Sam. 15:22-23; 1 Kings 11:9-12; 21:17-19; Isa. 63:1-6). Thus, this significant truth of Malachi is supported by well authenticated facts which come from Israel's previous history. Herein Israel's distinctive relationship to Yahweh is emphasized. Scott sees it as something that is not mediated on a mechanical basis but in a covenant with an intelligent, ethical, and personal character.[1] This is Israel's true identity and quality as a nation—the people of God. Acceptable response to the covenant is registered in obedience to Yahweh's will in social life, and faith in his power to save from calamity and to achieve his historic purpose.

THE DECLARATION THAT DIVINE LOVE THREATENS PUNISHMENT (2:1-3)

An Entreaty to Repent (2:1-2a)

2:1 And now, unto you is this commandment, O priests.
2a If you will not begin to hear, and if you will not lay it to heart, to give glory to my name, says Yahweh of hosts.

"And now, unto you is this commandment, O priests." The tone in this verse is judicial in nature, but it indicates that restraint is being exercised in the face of impending judgment. The unworthy conduct of the ministers at the altar had been declared and described as serious (cf. 1:6-14). It has to do with corrupt practices in worship and irreverence toward God.

No specific commandment is stated, but the sense of the context is that of burden or judgment. God's counsel, entreaty, and warning already had been given. But wrongdoing and cynical attitudes continued to prevail. In the language and spirit of Amos everything is being done, and all restraints are being exercised to avoid a personal confrontation with God and the visitation of the inevitable judgment (cf. Amos 4:4-12).

[1]Scott, *The Relevance of the Prophets,* pp. 139-40.

The priests are addressed because of their responsibility and knowledge as divinely appointed leaders. This does not excuse the people for their sin, but it magnifies the failure of the priests to give the right leadership and counsel. They were the teachers and mediators in divine worship (cf. 2:7; Ex. 28:1f.; Deut. 33:10). Hosea magnifies the tragic failure of the priests and the people. He says, "And it shall be like people, like priest; I will punish them for their ways, and requite them for their deeds" (cf. Hos. 4:9; 5:1; also Jer. 5:30-31). Joel calls on the priests to wail and to dress themselves in sackcloth, the symbol of humility, grief, and contrition (cf. 2:13). They are to involve the people in a fast and a solemn assembly at the house of God to entreat the Lord for his mercy (cf. Joel 2:14, 17; 1 Sam. 7:6). On account of this, Malachi arraigns the priests as first in worship and declares that they are first in sin and judgment.

The patience and mercy of God are emphasized in the condition which is declared in verse 2. Even when it appears that there is no further reason to delay, a respite is given (cf. Ex. 34:6-7). There is a call to repent as a means of staying the penalty (cf. Ps. 7:12). Thus the Lord declares through his prophet that failure to hearken and to lay the matter to heart will close the door to any further extensions of mercy (cf. Isa. 57:1; Dan. 1:8). To hearken means to hear with a mind or determination to obey. It is expressive of faith that bears the fruit of obedience. This is the kind of hearing which the Lord exacted of Israel in the making of the covenant (cf. Ex. 19:5-6). The call to lay it to heart marks the use of parallelism to emphasize the importance of the declaration. The term heart is not to be applied to the physical organ that pumps blood but to man's total being. It involves his intellect, emotions, and will (cf. Deut. 6:5).

The concern of the call to heartfelt obedience is to give glory or honor to the name of God in worship by offering the correct sacrifices and performing the right ritual. This can be done only by those who have a sincere spirit and a right attitude toward God. To give glory to God is to magnify or make great his name. It is that which is expressed by the psalmist in the depth of his being in blessing God's holy name (cf. Ps. 103:1-2). Jesus taught his disciples to pray "hallowed be thy name" (cf. Matt. 6:9). The fact that God is a great king and his name is being reverenced among the heathen should serve both to shame and to provoke Israel and the priests to obedience (cf. Mal. 1:11, 14).

The Punishment Described (2:2b-3)

Blessings Are to be Cursed (2:2b)

2:2b "... then I will send upon you the curse, and I will curse your blessings; yea I will curse them because you are not laying it to heart."

It has been pointed out that the priests were to pronounce a blessing upon the people as a part of their ministry (cf. Num. 6:24-26). The threatened curse is regarded by some to be a reversal of this privilege. This would be to make the work of the priest impotent and ineffective. The judgment of God upon Baalam is a striking example of this in reverse (cf. Num. 23:7-12; Neh. 13:12). A tragic judgment upon a priest would be to turn all of his attempted blessings into a curse. Every time he opened his mouth he would say, "The Lord curse you." An additional curse would be exercised in taking away the goods or material benefits of his office (cf. 3:10). The provisions which God made for the priests and Levites and their families are clearly specified in tithes and offerings and portions of the sacrifices which were brought to the altar (cf. Num. 18:3-32). The use of the definite article which calls attention to *the* curse may indicate a specified judgment (cf. Deut. 28:15-19). The last part of verse 2 may be translated in the future tense and would be in keeping with the first part of the verse. This translation would be a parallel statement for the purpose of emphasizing the solemn reality of the impending judgment. The future tense is regarded by some to be redundant and superfluous. To translate it "yea, I have cursed them because you are not laying it to heart" is taken to mean that the judgment is already in progress because there is no indication of repentance (cf. Jer. 6:16-20).

Disqualified for Service (2:3)

2:3 "Behold, I am rebuking your seed and I will spread dung upon your faces, the dung of your offerings, and I will take you away with it."

Several different translations are given. "I will corrupt your seed" (KJV). "I will rebuke your offspring" (RSV). "I will rebuke your seed" (ASV). "I will cut off the arm" (LXX). Some translate the word "arm" as "shoulder" and consider it to be a reference to the shoulder of the animal that was to be given to the priest as a part of his blessing (cf. Lev. 7:32; Deut. 18:3). The word seed may be applied to offspring (cf. Gen. 3:15; 12:7; 17:7-8). In this sense the curse would be extended to the children of the offenders (cf. Ex. 34:7; 1 Sam. 2:30-36). If it is made to apply to the seed which is planted in the fields, it would mean that there would be a crop failure caused by a drought or the rotting of the seed (cf. Joel 1:8-12; Hab. 3:17; Hag. 1:10-11). This sort of curse would affect the physical comforts and bring about a reduction of income. This would be true also if the translation, "I will withhold from you the shoulder" is accepted. To rebuke or cut off the arm would be to take away the priest's spiritual power to bless which is symbolized in the stretching forth of the hands. This latter meaning appears to fit the context when considering the rest of the threatened judgment: ". . . and I will spread dung upon your faces, the dung of your offerings, and I will take you away with it."

The dung is that which comes from the sacrificial animals. To add insult to injury, it is declared that the dung will be spread upon their faces. This will make the priests unclean and unfit for their priestly functions. This may be teaching and prophecy by drastic means in order to declare that the priesthood and the sacrificial system are going to come to an end (cf. Matt. 27:51). As they had offered unclean and polluted offerings that were unacceptable to the Lord, they themselves will be polluted, made unclean, impotent, and repudiated by him. This repudiation will be marked by their being taken away as dung is taken to the garbage dump (cf. Lev. 4:11f.). This is a pitiable plight. Their power with God and their influence over men are gone.

They are unfit vessels, disqualified to serve. This appears to be the fear expressed by the apostle Paul (cf. 1 Cor. 9:26-27). It is not a loss of salvation; it is a loss of usefulness.

THE COMMANDMENT AND THE COVENANT
EMPHASIZED (2:4-5)

2:4 And you shall know this commandment, that my covenant may prevail with Levi, says Yahweh of hosts.
5 My covenant was with him of life and peace; and I proceeded to give them to him (also) reverence, and he continually reverenced me, and before the face of my name, he bowed down.

Here the prophet makes reference to Levi, the priestly tribe, as a means of magnifying the high calling of the priesthood as a divine order and the consequences of failing to take its responsibilities seriously. The priesthood was founded on Levi. Malachi judges the religious leadership of his time by the example of Levi who was the divine pattern (cf. 2:4). Although a covenant of the priesthood is not definitely specified in the establishment of the office, the account of the covenant with Phinehas, the grandson of Aaron, provides some help (cf. Num. 25:12f.; Deut. 18:1-8; 33:8-11). This could have been a reference to a copy of the original covenant. Nehemiah refers to a covenant of the priesthood and the Levites (cf. 13:29). The knowledge which is referred to in connection with the covenant is the knowledge of experience which will be gained through the judgment which is soon to fall upon them for their failure to take the covenant seriously. "That my covenant with Levi may prevail" emphasizes the perpetual nature of the covenant and its binding obligation upon all who serve in the office of the priesthood. The covenant was just as authoritative in Malachi's time as it was when it was first given. It provided a binding of Yahweh and Levi in worship and service. The keeping of the covenant is the means by which the priest may be worthy of the office. It is by this that he abides in honor and usefulness with the assurance of the blessings of Yahweh. Thus the prevailing of the covenant guaranteed the prevailing of the office and those who served in it. This constituted both the authority of the priesthood and a responsible stewardship.

"My covenant was with him of life and peace, and I proceeded to give them to him (also) reverence, and he continually reverenced me." These terms are the stipulations or provisions of the covenant. It was a covenant of life, peace, and reverence. The Hebrew word for life which is employed here is plural with the meaning of "fullness." The same word is used in Genesis 2:7 which declares that God breathed into the nostrils of man the breath of lives, life in full measure. It also is employed with reference to the tree of life (cf. Gen. 2:9). The emphasis is on quality and not quantity. It is life that is divine in its origin and duration. It is characterized as spiritual, victorious, and satisfying. Its fullness is realized by doing God's will and feeding on his word (cf. Lev. 18:5; Deut. 32:46-47; Isa. 32:16-17). "Peace" (*shalom*) is the familiar Hebrew term of greeting and is expressive of all well-being. One who has peace has health, prosperity, security, salvation, and uprightness. It is a desired possession in life and in death (cf. Ps. 34:14; Isa. 38:17; Gen. 15:15).

Fear appears to be a gift of God as well as life and peace. Translators wrestle with this phrase, especially the word "fear." The KJV renders it "and I gave them to him for the fear wherewith he feared me." The ASV and RSV render it "and I gave them to him that he might fear, and he feared me." The LXX and Vulgate suggest, "and I gave to him fear." It is possible to regard life and peace to be the divine side of the covenant, and fear to be its human side. This is in accord with the KJV, RSV, and ASV translations. The LXX and Latin Vulgate are in accord with the Hebrew text and make all of these things gifts from God.

It is necessary to understand the term "fear." By some it is viewed as terror or flight, meaning that one is to be afraid of God. Its paramount meaning is awe, reverence, or honor. It is used of man's relationships both to God and to his fellowman. Man expresses his reverence for God in humility and loving obedience. Expressions of fear in the Old Testament are made significant by imperative force, promised rewards, and graphic illustrations. These things are clearly seen when their tracks are traced. The Book of Proverbs declares that "the fear of Yahweh is the head thing of knowledge" (cf. 1:7).

Fear may be the human response to the covenant, but if it is, it is something which man receives from God and exercises with regard to God's holiness, his name, his word, and all other relationships which he has with him. It may be concluded that the rich blessings of life, peace, and reverence are received from Yahweh and are to be the means of blessing all who are brought to share in them.

REVERENCE AND OBEDIENCE MAGNIFIED (2:6-7)

2:6 The law of truth was in his mouth, and unrighteousness was not found in his lips. He walked with me in peace and uprightness, and turned many from iniquity.

7 Because the lips of a priest should keep knowledge, and they (people) should continually seek instruction from his mouth; because he is the messenger of Yahweh of hosts.

The torah of truth, true instruction, was in his mouth, and unrighteousness was not found in his lips. This is a retrospect that looks at the portrait of the faithful performance of those who served in the priestly office. It is a worthy legacy which is given to all priests who succeed to the office. The honesty and integrity of the faithful priests in rendering judgments and imparting instruction are magnified. Here the ideal priest is praised for his moral integrity, not his ability to recite the ritual and to administer the sacrifices.

In all that was required of the priests in the fulfillment of their office, they were to be honest and righteous, walking in peaceful fellowship with God. Leading in worship is an art; teaching the word of God and rendering judgments are awesome responsibilities. One who accepts this stewardship should walk with God. Oracles or messages were to be secured from the Lord (cf. Ex. 28:30; Lev. 8:8-10; Num. 27:18-21; Deut. 17:8; 19:15-19; 33:8-11; 1 Sam. 14:36f.). These oracles were to be taught to the people (cf. Lev. 8:8; 10:11; Ezra 7:10). People were admonished to seek instruction from the Lord through the priest (cf. Deut. 17:9-11; 33:8-10; 1 Sam. 1:17; 22:10f.; 23:9-12).

It was said of the ideal priest that true instruction was in his mouth, and iniquity was not found in his lips. This is not to be applied to a written code of law but to oral decisions and pronouncements made by the priests. A primary function of his ministry was to teach and give counsel. The priests were assigned the responsibility of teaching the judgments and the laws of Yahweh to the people (cf. Ex. 18:20; Judg. 18:5; 1 Sam. 10:17; 22:13-15). They were commanded to give torah on matters of worship, juridical problems, and personal difficulties. The priest's decisions were just, providing deliverance for the poor and oppressed, and punishment for the disobedient and rebellious. Right judgments were assured because they came from God, and they were imparted through lips that were not marred by sin or false instruction. Scott observed:

> Though justice was administered according to custom and right by the elders, the formulation of civil laws was largely the work of the priests, often, apparently, under prophetic influence. The tradition of Moses was in their keeping, and the *mishpat,* or code, of the community had its source in the righteous will of the national God, who spoke through them.[1]

The ideal priest is further characterized by the fact that he walked with God in peace and uprightness and turned many away from all iniquity. To be able to walk is a blessing, but to walk with God is the greatest of all blessings. It is God's desire for all men to walk with him (cf. Deut. 13:4). A covenant to walk with God is life's greatest and most important decision and commitment (cf. 2 Kings 23:3). Such a covenant brings one into agreement with him and leads to a surrendered will (cf. Amos 3:3). It is a life of intimate fellowship in prayer and worship. One who walks with God can perform any service for him in a pleasing manner. It is said that Enoch and Noah walked with God (cf. Gen. 5:22-24; 6:9).

This way of life is characterized as one of peace and uprightness. The term "peace," discussed above, suggest completeness, soundness, and welfare (cf. Ps. 38:3; Isa. 38:17; Gen. 43:27; Ex. 18:7). It is a state of tranquility and contentment (cf. Isa. 32:17; 57:2). It is God's gift to those who

---

[1]*Ibid.,* p. 165.

are obedient to him (cf. Isa. 26:3; 27:5; Pss. 85:8-10; 119:165). Uprightness may be explained by the terms straight, smooth, or plain. As it pertains to God and things related to him, it is that which is righteous, well pleasing, or straightforward (cf. Ps. 119:128; Prov. 3:6; 11:5; Deut. 13:18; Hos. 14:9).

The power and influence of such a life bless the saints and turn many from iniquity. The proclamation of God's message, intercession, leadership in worship, and godly living find their highest fulfillment in turning people away from sin. A righteous life will do as much to silence the cynical and save sinners as all prophetic proclamation. This is the paramount need in every generation. The cause of the Lord and the Lord himself are brought into tragic disrepute when those who make no profession of religion have higher moral and ethical standards than his professed followers. The rewards of teaching and turning people from iniquity are made prominent by another prophet in his proclamation:

> And they that are causing others to be wise shall shine as the brightness of the firmament; and they that are causing many to turn to righteousness as the stars for ever and ever.— (Daniel 12:3, author's translation).

"Because the lips of a priest should guard knowledge." This is the only time the word "knowledge" is found in Malachi. The emphasis here continues the thought that is found in verse 6. It is concerned with the importance of the godly life, the high calling, and the awe-inspiring responsibility which should characterize all who would follow in Levi's train as God's true ministers.

It is here declared to be the responsibility of the priest to keep or to be the guardian of knowledge. This knowledge is more than that which is contained in the ritual and the ceremonial law—that which is outward and formal. It is not met in mere intellectual perception. The knowledge which he is to keep is that of a spiritual, intimate, experiential relationship with God (cf. Hos. 4:1; 6:6). It is the kind of knowledge that is marked by spiritual vitality and moral conduct. Hosea says, "My people are destroyed for lack of knowledge; because you have rejected knowledge, I reject you from being a priest to me. And since you have forgotten the law of your God, I also will forget your children" (cf. Hosea 4:6). The priest is not to keep knowledge in the sense of trying to hoard it or to protect it. Rather, he is to be a repository of the word of Yahweh where all who may desire can come and draw out its treasures new and old (cf. Ex. 28:29-30; Num. 27:21; Jer. 23:22; Neh. 8:8). This constitutes both a chilling and awesome responsibility and a thrilling and glorious opportunity. If one is to be a fountain of God's knowledge, he must live in daily contact with its source, enlarge the cells of his heart and mind to contain it, and seek to sharpen all of his faculties for the purpose of effectively dispensing it.

People should continually seek instruction from the mouth of the priest. People as used here is an all inclusive term. It closes the door to no one, because God is available to all. Everyone is invited and urged to seek the instruction which is made available by the Lord (cf. Isa. 55:1ff.; Rev. 20:17). The admonition to seek instruction presupposes man's supreme need for it, his ability to receive it, and his desire to have it. The amount which one may have is limited only by his desire. The laws of supply and demand are mutually inclusive. To be able to impart instruction for God is man's greatest responsibility and blessing. The teaching function of the priest is emphasized and the importance of what he teaches is made prominent, because he is the messenger of Yahweh of hosts. He gives instruction regarding redemption, godliness, and God's will. Failure to hear and obey the instruction which he gives will meet with severe judgment from God (cf. Deut. 17:10-13). This is the only time the title angel or messenger is applied to the priest in the Old Testament (unless Ecclesiastes 5:6 is taken to be an exception.) Some interpreters consider this emphasis to be an indication that the priest is divinely commissioned to take over the office of the prophet. Prophets are called Yahweh's messengers (cf. Hag. 1:13; Mal. 1:1). "Messenger" also is used to designate the angel of Yahweh, the pre-incarnate manifestation of Christ in the Old Testament, who appeared to many people on numerous occasions to reveal God and to proclaim his message (cf. Gen. 16:7; 22:11-12; Ex. 3:2; 23:20-23; Judg. 2:1-5; 12:8ff.). Thus the priest as God's messenger is a part of an exalted and meaningful fellowship.

The above conclusions reveal that the intellectual duties of the ministry constitute an awesome responsibility. A minister with a trained mind is the delight of his parishioners and a vital asset to Christianity and the world. There is a faithful priesthood of knowledge and instruction. Both of these things require study and skills. If they are to be pursued, it is essential to have time and tools with an impelling sense of duty that drives one to his task. By the maxim "much study is a weariness of the flesh" (Eccl. 12:12) many would have little reason to be weary. A poor stewardship of intellect in the ministry may be the reason that some never feel any urge to worship God or to become a part of the company of the committed. It could be a contributing factor in the birth and growth of many religious *-isms* which prevail among us. Failure to study and teach the whole counsel of God is a deadly peril, both to the minister and to the community of believers whom he seeks to lead.

PUNISHMENT JUSTIFIED (2:8-9)

2:8 "But you yourselves have turned aside from the way; you have caused many to stumble by the instruction; you have perverted the covenant of Levi," says Yahweh of hosts.

9 "Now I myself also have made you despised and contemptible before all the people, inasmuch as you are not guarding my ways, but you are keeping on showing partiality in the instruction."

The sin and failure of the priests of Malachi's time are silhouetted upon a background of the ideal priesthood of another day. The priests cared for the welfare of the people, made intercession, lived exemplary lives, and honored God. They imparted the instruction as it was given to them and performed their duties in humble reverence before God. This is an idealistic appraisal of the work of the priests. It magnifies the best that was within them. It appears that a mantle of charity was thrown over their weaknesses and failures by the prophet in order to magnify the sins of the people to whom he preached. This may be regarded as teaching by exaggeration in order to make a particular emphasis prominent and forceful. But this appraisal was merited by the faithful among the priests who had been God's true ministers. They declared his counsel, rendered his judgments, and turned many from iniquity. Malachi charges the priests of his day with the sin of turning aside from the way. They were the very opposite of the above characterization. They aided improper worship and merited the accusation of being false and unworthy spiritual leaders. Herbert has observed:

> A sacrifice offered by one who was indifferent to Yahweh's claims upon his life effected no communion with God (Prov. 15:8, 21:27). It is sacrifice without a desire for righteousness or a devotion to the covenant relationship that earns the prophet's condemnation.[1]

Malachi does not say exactly what the way is, but it is to be assumed that he is referring to the way of life, peace, reverence, and uprightness which marked the steps of Levi, and for which he received commendation (cf. 2:5-6). In their turning aside from the way, many were caused to stumble. Such a way of life is condemned by a writer of the Proverbs (cf. 4:14-16). This scandal or stumbling block was brought about by wrong or perverted teaching. It was marked by partiality. The priests failed to give the instruction that would guide the people to the Lord. Their walk was in forbidden paths that set the wrong example. Thus the people that should have been a help were a hindrance. They invited the judgment of the Almighty because of their failure to perform the service which was required of them (cf. Deut. 33:10).

A stumbling block is a hurdle, an obstacle, or an offense. The religious leadership caused perplexity, contributed to wrong-doing, and became an impediment to acceptable worship. In these ways the covenant of Levi was perverted. Thus the covenant, designed for mutual fellowship and blessing (cf. 2:6-7), is annulled by false dealing and broken promises. Such had been true of some of the priests of former times. They had

---

[1]A. S. Herbert, *Worship in Ancient Israel*, Ecumenical Studies in Worship (Richmond: John Knox Press, 1965), p. 22.

been challenged and condemned (cf. Amos 4:4-5; 5:21-26; 7:14-17; 9:1; Hos. 4:4-6; 5:1; 6:7-10; Isa. 1:11-16; Mic. 1:5-7). Even Aaron, the high priest, led the whole nation into idolatry, repudiating Yahweh and the covenant (cf. Ex. 32:1ff.). He and Miriam sought to discredit the leadership of Moses because of their jealousy and selfishness (cf. Num. 12:1-5). Korah led 250 Levites in an effort to gain power and leadership which did no longer belong to them (cf. Num. 16:1ff.). Nadab and Abihu were judged because of their sin (cf. Num. 16:1ff.). Nadab and Abihu were judged because of their sin (cf. Lev. 10:1ff.). Eli and his two sons were unfaithful to their trust and were set aside by the Lord (cf. 1 Sam. 2:27ff.). Here are illustrations from history. They confirm the fact that disobedience will meet with just retribution.

In discussing the hereditary relationships of the priestly office, Rowley observed:

There was always the initial privilege and opportunity of the inheritance, but if responsibility and opportunity were cast aside, the privilege was turned into a burden of guilt.[1]

Rowley further declared:

The Biblical doctrine of election is therefore penetrated through and through with warning. To be the elect of God is not to be His favourite. It is to be challenged to a loyalty and a service and a sacrifice that knows no limits, and to feel the constraint of the Divine love to such a degree that no response can seem adequate and no service worthy. The constraint is not of our choosing. It is laid upon us. We can resist it, but if we do so resist it we act disgracefully. For we have received of the grace of God, and its obligation already lies upon us.[2]

The impending judgment is not without warning and precedent. "Now I myself also have made you despised and contemptible before all the people" is the oracle of the Lord. This is a solemn declaration and a serious judgment. The priests and their work are despised. The people whom they sought to lead and who were to seek instruction from their lips

[1] Rowley, *The Biblical Doctrine of Election*, p. 103.

[2] *Ibid.*, p. 168.

had no confidence in their instruction and leadership, because they were no more worthy of respect and trust. Those who were guilty of despising the Lord and his work meet with the same judgment. The words "despised and contemptible" constitute the biography of a delinquent leadership that has become detestable. It is the undeniable fact of faulty character giving birth to foolish conduct and reaping the fatal consequences (cf. Gen. 25:27-34; 27:34-38; Ezek. 7:26).

The verb used to describe the judgment is that significant previous present that sees a thing as already started in the past and continuing in the present. One who is despised is regarded with contempt. The term base is a synonym for contemptible. It has the sense of humiliation or abasement. The serious import of this lack of trust is magnified by the fact that it is the consensus of all the people. It was no longer contained within the limited circles of the priesthood with a mild rebuke (cf. 1 Sam. 2:22-26). It is in the hands of the Lord who purposes to see that it meets with just retribution.

"Inasmuch as you are not guarding my ways, but you keep on showing partiality in the law" are the reasons declared for the judgment which has come. It was the responsibility of the priests to keep God's ways for themselves and to make them available and strive to make them effective in their ministry to the people. God's laws which were to be applied in the adjudication of disputes which were brought before the priests by the people were not always adhered to. Partiality was being shown either on the basis of friendship or for financial consideration (cf. Micah 3:11; Zeph. 3:4; Ezek. 22:26). The word "partial" is the translation of the Hebrew term which means to lift up or show respect for faces. The emphasis is on favoring unjustly. The use of the present active participle describes a continuous, never ending practice. The text does not state to whom or exactly why partiality was being shown. It is to be supposed that it was extended to those who had special distinction either by official position, social standing, or wealth (cf. Jas. 2:1ff.). That some kind of advantage, financial or otherwise, was provided for the priest for his partiality in judgment would be a valid assumption. The reality of such a practice in any sphere of life is a serious indictment. It is sharply condemned in the Scriptures (cf. Ps. 82:2-4; Deut. 1:17; 10:17-18; Amos 2:6-7; Jas. 2:1). The price for such conduct is high, and it is tragic when there are those who are willing to be ruled by lust and greed in order to obtain what such base appetites desire (cf. Hos. 1:8; 14; 14:9).

A fitting conclusion to this sad burlesque and debacle is verbalized in graphic word pictures:

> The language in which Malachi depicts the fate of the religious leaders is incredibly drastic. What lashes the prophet to fury is that ideal to which these ministers of religion have proved recreant is so lovely. Nowhere are the duty and dignity of a true minister of God more winsomely described than in vv. 5-7, and every minister should test himself by this description.[1]

[1]John E. McFadyen, *Old Testament Scenes and Characters* (London: James Clarke and Company, 1928), p. 202.

V. Divine Love Despises Unfaithfulness

This section of the prophecy is judged to be one of the most difficult portions of the book. The major problems which are confronted by the interpreter are linguistic and contextual. The translation difficulties are related particularly to verses 11, 12, and 15. After settling on a translation, the meaning of some of the terms remains somewhat obscure. The term which is translated "sanctuary" is also translated "holiness" (cf. vs. 11). Both translations may be justified, but they lead to different interpretations. Verse 12 remains an enigma even after it has passed through the sieve of many interpreters. Weeping takes place, but who is doing it and why? (cf. vs. 13).

It should be observed that this portion of the text introduces a new theme. After dealing with the worship of the people with particular emphasis on the priestly covenant, the prophet turns to the serious domestic problem of the divorce of Hebrew wives and marriage to heathen women. This is another example of covenant breaking and the repudiation of the love of Yahweh concerning which the people had expressed their doubts (cf. 1:2). It is like a malignant disease that threatened to destroy their language, worship, family structure, and national unity (cf. Deut. 18:9-14). In a sense the prophet makes a surprise attack by asking the questions and then proceeding to answer them.

UNFAITHFULNESS DEFINED (2:10-11)

Profaning the Covenant of the Fathers (2:10)

2:10 Is there not one father of all of us? Did not one God create us? Why do we deal unfaithfully every man with his brother, to profane the covenant of our fathers?

The prophet is emphasizing the fact of the unity of the Hebrew family in these two questions. The second question, following the Hebrew pattern of parallelism, gives the answer to the first one. The father about whom he speaks is God who has created them. This makes irrelevant any references to Adam, Abraham, or Jacob as a possible answer to the first question. The context makes it clear that the emphasis is on Israel as a distinct and separate people (cf. Deut. 7:3-4, 6; 32:18; Isa. 63:16; Jer. 3:19). God created them as individuals and as a nation. He chose them as his peculiar treasure from among all peoples and created a covenant that specified mutual obligations. He created laws which were designed to protect these covenant relations and to make them "a kingdom of priests and a holy nation." He created their opportunities and responsibilities. He created the providences by which they had been protected and sustained. He created their land and placed them in it. This does not mean that God did not create all mankind, but this is not the concern of the prophet here. The common brotherhood of the nation is a cogent argument against unbrotherly acts. God's election love brought the nation together in a common bond and for a common purpose. This made possible a new existence and a new unity whereby the universal fatherhood of God and the brotherhood of man could be anticipated as a glorious reality (cf. Gen. 12:1-3; Ex. 19:5-6; Isa. 19:23-25).

The prophet's understanding and appreciation of the unique relationship of the nation to the great God of the universe led him to ask, "Why do we deal unfaithfully every man with his brother, to profane the covenant of our fathers?" Treacherous dealing which is out of character with the family relationships is the meaning here. The family unit expresses the ideal structure of the nation. Failure to meet the obligations involved in this relationship is to court disaster. The serious nature of the offense to which he refers and which he discusses later (cf. vss. 11-13) involves the profaning of the covenant.[1] Arguments against reference to any specific covenant are not valid because of the use of covenantal terminology both for the covenant itself and the profanation which characterized its violation (cf. Pss. 55:20; 89:31-34). This verse forms a vital connection with the context, and its meaning must be sought in verses 11-16. Malachi makes a charge which he says involves "the covenant of our fathers." This could hardly be any other than the covenant which marked their election as a nation and separated them from all others (cf. Ex. 19:5-6; 24:8; Amos 3:2). This covenant is not to be confused with the one mentioned in verse 8 nor with the marriage covenant which also was violated (cf. vs. 14, also Gen. 2:24). The covenant with the nation which separated Israel from all others imposed restraints regarding foreigners, including marriage (cf. Ex. 34:10-16; Deut. 7:3-4).

Profaning the Sanctuary of the Lord (2:11)

2:11 Judah has been faithless, and an abomination has been done in Israel and in Jerusalem; because Judah has profaned the holy place (sanctuary) of Yahweh which he loves, and has married the daughter of a foreign god.

The whole nation is indicted for the sin, and it is involved in the consequences by the declaration that Judah has been faithless, and an abomination has been done in Israel and in Jerusalem. The faithlessness or treacherous dealing is repeated here from verse 10 for emphasis. The new element which is

[1] J. M. P. Smith, Ward and Bewer, *A Critical and Exegetical Commentary on the Book of Malachi*, p. 48.

introduced is abomination and evidently refers to things which excite disgust and hatred (cf. Deut. 7:25-26; 17:2-5; 27:15; 1 Kings 11:5-7; Ezek. 8:9-13; Prov. 6:16-19).

A textual problem is seen in the phrase "in Israel and in Jerusalem." Smith regarded it to have been placed in the text by an editor. He observed that Israel is not distinguished from Judah anywhere else in Malachi. To consider Israel as identical with Judah here would hardly be appropriate because of the use of Judah in the beginning verse.[1] Hailey considered Judah to be a reference to the nation as a whole and Israel as the covenant name "providing a contrast between what the people were and what they should have been."[2]

The abomination which has befallen the whole nation has come because Judah has profaned the holy place of Yahweh which he loves. The term "holy place," also translated "sanctuary," is thought to be a reference to the temple, God's dwelling place (cf. 1 Kings 8:12; 2 Chron. 29:5; Ezek. 5:11). It could be profaned by the presence of unconsecrated objects or people, including a foreigner of heathen religion. The Holiness Code reveals the fact that the sanctuary is profaned by the sin of the people (cf. Lev. chs. 17-26). The translation (KJV), "the holiness of the Lord," has been applied to the temple, the covenant, and to Israel as a holy nation, God's holy people whom he loves (cf. 1:2; Ex. 19:6; Deut. 14:2; Isa. 57:15; Jer. 2:3; Ezra 9:2; Ps. 47:4).

It appears to be in keeping with the context of Malachi to regard the temple as the thing which is profaned. The profanation of the holy place is said to be because Judah has married the daughter of a foreign god. An allegorical interpretation, which takes unusual liberties with the text, makes some rather incredible applications. It regards the divorce of Yahweh and marriage to heathen gods to be the meaning of the passage. Key words are associated with heathen ritual. The daughter of a foreign god is taken to mean a foreign cult. The wife of Israel's

[1]*Ibid.*

[2]Homer Hailey, *A Commentary on the Minor Prophets* (Grand Rapids: Baker Book House, 1972), p. 415.

youth is said to be Yahweh. Covering the altar with tears is associated with Tammuz worship (cf. Ezek. 8:14). "Putting away" is taken to mean the stripping of one's body in pagan rites. It has been admitted that there are serious textual problems in this passage which are puzzling and which make it difficult to understand and interpret. However, to put pagan content into all of the key words seems farfetched. There is no clear precedent in the Scriptures for this interpretation.

It has been suggested that the sense in Malachi is that an alliance has been made between Judah and people who do not worship Yahweh through their marriage to the daughter of a foreign god. Any alliance of the people of Yahweh with foreign nations was opposed by the prophets. They regarded such relationships as an indication of Israel's lack of trust in Yahweh, disloyalty to him, and as a means of introducing idolatry into the nation (cf. Hosea 7:11; 8:8ff.; Isa. 18:1ff.). [1]

To regard this passage as a strong pronouncement against intermarriage with heathen women seems more natural. This interpretation has history in its favor (cf. Deut. 7:3-4, 25-26; 1 Kings 11:1ff.; 16:29ff.). Ezra and Nehemiah, contemporaries of Malachi, condemned mixed marriages (cf. Ezra 9-10; Neh. 13:23-28). These passages could not be taken to mean anything except intermarriage with heathen women. They give no support to the allegorical view that they were marrying heathen gods nor that an alliance was being made with foreign people. It should be stated here that the way Ezra and Nehemiah handled the problem is not without question. That intermarriage with heathen women opened the doors of the homes of the people of Judah to idolatry and encouraged such worship is an undeniable fact. Even in our generation some mixed marriages, where there are different or no religious affiliations, have created serious domestic and religious problems. Paul's admonition not to be unequally yoked together with unbelievers may be applicable here (cf. 2 Cor. 6:14).

"He has married the daughter of a foreign god" is the solemn declaration of the prophet regarding Judah. The marriage is to

[1] J. M. P. Smith, Ward and Bewer, *A Critical and Exegetical Commentary on the Book of Malachi*, p. 49.

a foreign woman who worships a foreign or a heathen deity. Malachi does not identify the country or countries from which these women came. There are many possibilities. Some of Solomon's wives came from Egypt, Moab, Ammon, Edom, and Sidon (cf. 1 Kings 11:1). Nehemiah, in Malachi's time, identifies the women whom the Jews were marrying as being from Ashdod (Philistia), Ammon, and Moab. He points to Solomon's sin in this matter as a warning against such apostasy (cf. Neh. 13:23-27). The practice appears to be widespread. It had become a national problem that threatened to destroy Yahweh worship. The motivation for these marriages could have been wealth, political advantage, children, or sexual lust.

The spiritual relationship between God and his people is figuratively portrayed by the prophets as a betrothal and marriage (cf. Isa. 62:4-5; Hos. 2:19). Unfaithfulness to the marital relationship by a wife is used to illustrate the meaning of apostasy through idolatry (cf. Isa. 1:21; Jer. 3:1ff.; Hos. 2:1ff.). Worshippers of the one true God in Israel are called sons and daughters of Yahweh (cf. Deut. 14:1; 32:19; Isa. 1:2; Hos. 1:10; 11:1). In the same way, one who worships a heathen god is considered to be a son or a daughter of that deity (cf. Num. 21:29; Deut. 32:10; Jer. 2:27). It has been pointed out that foreign marriages were a serious threat to the Hebrew faith, a contamination of home life, and an undermining of moral and ethical stamina (cf. Neh. 13:23ff.).

UNFAITHFULNESS TO MEET WITH SEVERITY (2:12-17)

The people are threatened with severe punishment for their sin of mixed marriages. Every effort is made, however, to bring the people to repentance, thereby averting the punishment.

The Guilty to be Cut Off (2:12)

2:12 Let Yahweh cut off, to the man who does this, any to witness or answer from the tents of Jacob, and one bringing an offering to Yahweh.

The words of this verse are difficult because the Hebrew is ambiguous, and their meaning is obscure. The KJV translation is "the master and the scholar." The ASV translation is "him that waketh and him that answereth." The RSV renders it "any to witness or answer." These terms are considered by some interpreters to be a proverbial expression signifying that all the family of those who are involved in the transgression will be cut off; none will be left. If any one attempts to make an offering for the sin of the guilty, he will be cut off, too. The latter has been applied to the priests who are said to have been guilty of marital infidelity also. A more natural conclusion is to regard cutting off to be excommunication which would deprive the guilty one of his rights in court with no defender and his privileges in worship which include the ministry and advantages of the temple. This is in keeping with the judgment upon sins of presumption, those which are done with a high hand. Idolatry was in this category. The penalty which is exercised points to the heinous nature of the sin.

Offerings To Be Rejected (2:13)

2:13 And this again you do. You cover with tears the altar of Yahweh weeping and groaning, because he no longer has regard unto the offering, or to receive anything favorably from your hand.

Several meanings have been offered for a thing which is viewed as being repeated or done a second time. A second outbreak of marital infidelity has been suggested. It also has been applied to divorce, the first sin being the marriage to a heathen woman. The context suggests that the thing which was being done again was their covering the altar with tears. Some have applied this to the divorced wives who are come to the altar to weep and plead their cause before the Lord. This interpretation cannot be defended because women were not permitted to come to the altar. It is more natural and in keeping with the context to see this as a frequent outbreak of emotions by the guilty husbands. Again and again they went to the altar to wail and groan to see if they could awaken the compassion of God.

It is said that the Lord heard and answered the prayers of Hezekiah, taking note of his tears (cf. 2 Kings 20:5). Jeremiah yearned for his eyes to be a fountain of tears as an expression of his compassion for Israel (cf. Ps. 39:12). There is a marked distinction between the above examples and the weeping of the men of Malachi's time. The former were characterized by genuine penitence and sincerity, while the latter were counterfeit and hypocritical.

"Because he no longer has regard unto the offering, or to receive anything favorably from your hand" is the reason for the display of their emotion. The people did not weep over their sin—they wept because their outward forms of worship were not accepted by the Lord and did not bring his blessing.

The Work of Yahweh the God of
Justice (2:14-17)

Witnessing Wrongdoing (2:14)

> **2:14 Now you ask, "Why does he not?" Because Yahweh is witness between you and between the wife of your youth with whom you have been faithless, and she is your companion and the wife of your covenant.**

Here the prophet gives his forthright and incisive response as to why Yahweh did not answer the prayers of the people as they desired even though they were accompanied by weeping and groaning. It is because Yahweh is witness between them and the wife of their youth with whom they have been faithless. In discussing marriage, Paterson said:

> It is a divine ordinance and covenant that binds a man to his wife, and that covenant is no less sacred and indissoluble than the covenant that binds man to God. This is indeed high doctrine, and it finds its closest parallel in Paul's word in Ephesians 5:28ff.[1]

It is their sin which had closed the ears of God and stopped the channels of prayer (cf. Isa. 59:1-2; Jas. 4:3). It is possible

---

[1] John Paterson, *The Goodly Fellowship of the Prophets* (New York: Charles Scribner's Sons, 1948), p. 253.

for sinners to refuse to repent even though they may weep, make offerings, attend worship services, and perform charitable deeds. Indeed, these things may become a substitute for repentance or righteousness (cf. 1 Sam. 15:22-23; Ps. 51:16-17; Isa. 1:18-20; Amos 5:21-25; Mic. 6:6-8). The Lord, speaking through another prophet, diagnoses the case and offers the cure when he says,

"Yet even now," says the Lord, "return to me with all your heart, with fasting, with weeping, and with mourning; and rend your hearts and not your garments." Return to the Lord, your God, for he is gracious and merciful, slow to anger, and abounding in steadfast love, and repents of evil. (Joel 2:12-13).

Malachi declares that the marital infidelity was sin which was known to Yahweh, because he was the witness to the covenant between "you and the wife of your youth, to whom you have been faithless, and she is your companion and the wife of your covenant." This is a court scene in which Yahweh is the plaintiff, the witness, and the judge. The witness comes to the stand and accuses the one who is arraigned of marital infidelity. The marriage which was dissolved was consummated in the tender, youthful years of the contracting parties in the formal ceremony of a solemn covenant before God who had ordained the rite of marriage.

This covenant is now broken with no regard for love, the long years of faithful companionship, the worship of the one true God, or his disapproval of their treachery. All of the above considerations were set aside when the little heathen beauty came tripping along (cf. Prov. 5:15-23). According to earlier Jewish practices involving marriage, there would be no problem in taking another wife. This wide-spread practice, however, was never approved by the Lord (cf. Gen. 2:24; Deut. 24:1; Matt. 5:27-32). The objectionable features in this transaction are the twofold sin of the divorce of Hebrew wives and the marriage to heathen women. Right decisions and commitments which are made in youth are not to be repudiated in the evil times that may come in the advancing years.

The wives were set aside and silenced, but God is present and vocal in their behalf. When Hebrew men entered into marital relationships in their youth, God was present as a witness to the solemn covenant in which they pledged their troth that bound them to their wives for life (cf. Gen. 2:24; 31:50; Ezek. 16:8; Prov. 2:17).

Desiring Godly Offspring (2:15)

2:15 And did not he make one even though he had the Spirit? And why one? He was seeking a godly seed. Therefore take heed to your spirit and let not one continue to deal unfaithfully with the wife of his youth.

Critical scholars agree that this is one of the most difficult and obscure verses in the entire Old Testament. There are several possibilities in the translation of the text, and none of them is without its problems. Translations and interpretations alike vary widely.

The application of this verse to Abraham appears to have had wide acceptance at one time. It requires considerable imagination to work out the theory that is set forth concerning Abraham, Sarah, and Hagar. "And did not one do it? and he had a remnant of spirituality." This translation is offered and applied to Abraham. "A remnant of spirituality" is the meaning which is given to "the residue of the Spirit." If Abraham set Sarah aside because she was barren, what is wrong if we do it? This argument is taken to be the reasoning of the Jews as they sought to defend their actions against Malachi's preaching. This theory then has the prophet agreeing that Abraham did divorce Sarah. But Abraham's reason for such drastic action was in order to have godly offspring. It was not to gratify sexual lust.

The references to Abraham as "one" in Isaiah 51:2 and Ezekiel 33:24 are used here in a subtle twisting of the Scriptures in eisegesis to make them support a preconceived opinion. A reading of these verses will reveal that they speak of Abraham as "one" in the sense of his being only one person from whom the whole nation had come. "One" is never used as another name for Abraham.

The Genesis story in chapters 16-21 gives no support to the above theory. This account reveals that Sarah planned for Abraham to take Hagar, the Egyptian maiden who was their household servant, and raise up children through her as a means of fulfilling the promise of God for children. Abraham and Hagar were never married, nor was Sarah divorced. Hagar was the one who was sent away. God was not honored in or pleased with what took place. The seed which he promised was given at a later time in the birth of Isaac to Abraham and Sarah.

Another translation or paraphrase of the first part of the verse is "and no one has done it who has the residue of the Spirit or a remnant of spirituality." This makes for an entirely different interpretation. On the basis of the theory that applies this to Abraham, it could be used to prove that Abraham did not do what the Jews of Malachi's time were doing.

A more natural interpretation sees God as one who in the beginning created one man and one woman and ordained the rite of marriage. The implication is that God had the spirit of life and could have given Adam several wives if he had desired to do so. Monogamy was his intent, however, and it was in order to raise up a godly seed for a covenant people (cf. Gen. 1:27-28; 2:21-24; Ps. 127:3; Deut. 7:3-4, 6). To be intermarried with idolatrous people is to defeat God's purpose. It would give place to the forces that would destroy national distinctiveness, monotheistic worship, and godly living. Godly children do not ordinarily come from an atmosphere of strife, immorality, and ungodliness.

"Therefore take heed to your spirit and let not one continue to deal unfaithfully with the wife of his youth." The conclusion of the prophet is an exhortation to the people to let more seasoned judgment and spiritual character take control as a means of putting a stop to wife divorcing and marriages to heathen women. When God is allowed to have the reins of one's life, one cannot continue to practice unfaithfulness or wrongdoing.

Condemning Divorce and Skepticism (2:16-17)

2:16 "For he hates putting away," says Yahweh the God of Israel, "and him who covers his garment with violence,"

says Yahweh of hosts; wherefore take heed to your spirit and do not continually deal unfaithfully.

17 You have caused Yahweh to be weary with your words. Yet you say, "Wherein have we wearied him?" In your saying, all workers of evil are good in the eyes of Yahweh, and in them he takes delight; or where is the God of justice?

Verse 16 is a continuation and a partial repetition of verse 15. " 'For he hates putting away,' says Yahweh the God of Israel" is strong language. The word God is a generic term for deity which denotes magnitude, fullness, power, and transcendence. It is to be noted that this is the only time Malachi employs this title for God. A footnote in the Hebrew text suggests, "for I hate" instead of "he hates." This marks another use of the word hate in describing God's attitude toward sin and sinners (cf. 1:3). That which God is said to hate is "putting away . . . and him who covers his garment with violence . . . ." In this context, putting away is correctly interpreted to mean divorce. The significance of marriage and marital fidelity has been considered. This is the strongest pronouncement in the Old Testament against divorce and marital infidelity. It moves beyond Deuteronomy 24:1-4, blazing the trail and anticipating the teaching of Jesus and his proclamation in Matthew 5:27-32. According to Deuteronomy a man could divorce his wife for some indecency or a thing of nakedness (cf. 24:1). Divorce was allowed for a man in a patriarchal society. A woman had no such privilege. The provision which Moses made was on account of the hardness of the hearts of the people, but from the beginning it was not so (cf. Gen. 2:24; Mark 10:2-9). In spite of the fact that God hates divorce, the law of Moses provided some regulations and protection for women in the prohibition of promiscuous, hasty action (cf. Deut. 22:19, 29; 24:1-4).

Malachi ignores Moses and paints the beauty of monogamy over the sordid picture of divorce and declares God's hatred of it without any qualification. "And him who covers his garment with violence" magnifies the shame of divorce and indicts the guilty party. This appears to be a figure of speech and a symbolic portrayal of the wrong which is condemned. The term is not found elsewhere in the Old Testament. It may be related to an ancient custom among the Jews which was associated with courtship and marriage (cf. Deut. 22:30; Ruth 3:9; Ezek. 16:8). The details of this custom and its significance have been lost to us.

Some interpreters have regarded the garment to be a synonym for a man's wife. It may refer to the man himself. If the background which is given above is considered, a garment covered with violence may be taken to mean that the marriage relationship is treated with contempt and ends in divorce. The admonition of the prophet that was given in verse 15 is repeated here for emphasis. Varied opinions and views on 2:10-16 are presented by Eli Cashdan, I. G. Matthews, and J. M. P. Smith.[1]

Earlier in the text (cf. 1:13) it is declared that the people were weary with worship (church going) and all of its requirements. Now the prophet says "you have caused Yahweh to be weary" (cf. Isa. 43:24). The people interrupt or respond to the charge of the prophet in their usual style with the words, "wherein have we wearied you?" They desire to know more about the complaint.

This is an indication that the debate is still on. The spirit of skepticism, sarcasm, and self-justification prevails. The prophet's response to their "wherein?" is, "In your saying, all workers of evil are good in the eyes of Yahweh, and in them he himself delights; or where is the God of justice?" These people were among those who doubted that God was in control, and they labeled him as unfair. Malachi, like the prophets of the exile, declared that the judgment which had befallen them was God's doing, and it was just. They were suffering for their own sins, a thing which they needed to recognize for their own welfare (cf. Jer. 16:10-13; Ezek. 14:12-23; cf. also Isa. 42:24-25; 48:17-19). Their words indicate a sharp reaction to and a vicious condemnation of the prophet's preaching as well as a rejection of the God whose message he proclaims. The response of the people reveals their brute nature and their unwillingness to face

[1] Cashdan, "Malachi," pp. 345-48; Matthews, "Haggai, Malachi," pp. 21-28; and J. M. P. Smith, *Commentary on the Book of Malachi*, pp. 47-61.

reality. This is none other than the confusion of moral price tags and a parody of deism. It is a declaration that God either has no interest in morals, or he is too weak to visit judgment on the wicked. Isaiah describes such people in the words "Let him make speed, let him hasten his work, that we may see it; and let the counsel of the Holy One of Israel draw nigh and come, that we may know it!" (cf. Isa. 5:19; Eccl. 8:11; 2 Pet. 3:4). In this they maligned God's character and presumed on his patience.

This is a charge that God is like a man who winds a clock and lets it run down or starts a motor and lets it run until it is out of fuel. He has no interest in direction, consequences, or destiny. Such an application in human affairs means that evil is unchecked and good is unrewarded. This is a brazen and cynical denial of God's justice and righteousness in his government of the world. The dominant philosophy is that the righteous could claim no benefit or advantage over the unrighteous. This kind of reasoning made religious observances an empty farce and gave birth to all kinds of religious and moral corruption. This appears to be a part of the long struggle with the problem of the prosperity of the wicked and the privations and sufferings of the righteous (Ps. 37:1ff.; 73:1ff.; Jer. 12:1f.; Hab. 1:13; Ecc. 9:2-3). The argument of the people is that they were being penalized for being righteous.

It is no wonder that God is weary with such words. Their cynical charges, worthless promises, big talk, and godless living caused him to be tired of them and their words (cf. 1:12, 14; 2:8).

VI. Divine Love Personally Manifested

THROUGH THE MESSENGER OF THE COVENANT (3:1)

The Lord meets the challenge which the cynics hurled at him (cf. 2:17). He proceeds to manifest himself as the God of justice who will correct the inequities and injustices which were prevalent among his people (cf. Isa. 5:12). Malachi is here declaring what his predecessor enunciated when he said:

For the Lord will rise up as on Mount Perazim, he will be wroth as in the valley of Gibeon; to do his deed—strange is his deed! and to work his work—alien in his work!

Now therefore do not scoff, lest your bonds be made strong; for I have heard a decree of destruction from the Lord God of hosts upon the whole land. (Isaiah 28:21-22).

Skepticism and unbelief constituted a challenge to the covenant keeping God to show himself and to do his work.

His Coming To Be Heralded by
His Messenger (3:1a)

3:1a Behold, I am sending my messenger.
The use of the word "Behold" is a means of emphasizing that something startling and unusual is on the verge of taking place. It has an element of mystery and commands attention. The use of the present active participle—"am sending—indicates that something is being set in motion that will keep on going without interruption until it is accomplished. It is a continuous, unfailing thing that God is going on doing. This is eschatological language. The coming of the Lord is imminent. His judgment is about to take place in a unique way. This well may be associated with the day of Yahweh which is emphasized by Malachi's predecessors (cf. Obad. 17-21; Joel 1:15; 2:1-11; Amos 5:18-20). The popular opinion among the Jews was that this would be a day of blessing, deliverance, and victory over all of their enemies. Although this was a popular and widely accepted opinion in Israel, it is not exactly the way the prophets understood and applied it. A reading of Amos 3:2 and 5:18-20 and Joel 2:1-3 will reveal that sinners in Israel are to be judged also. This is likewise the concept of Malachi. Neglect and defiance of the will of Yahweh always have met with chastisement and sometimes disaster. God's judgments do not determine man's way. But they may become occasions for his obedient response and the ordering of his life in righteousness.

One called "my messenger" is being sent in advance of the coming of the Lord. The term "my messenger" is a translation of the Hebrew word "Malachi." The word messenger may be translated "angel." It is significant that the Lord dispatched one from that celestial group from time to time to convey his message to men. Prophets, both canonical and non-canonical, were messengers of the Lord (cf. 1 Sam. 2:27ff.; Hag. 1:13). Priests also were called messengers (cf. Mal. 2:7). The messenger in the text before us has a distinctive role in that his work is to prepare for the coming of the Lord. The problem for the interpreter is to identify this messenger. Malachi does not say who he is, where he is from, nor when he will come. Some have considered him to be the angel of Yahweh or that prophet like unto Moses (cf. Gen. 16:7; Deut. 18:18-19). A succession of prophets and a play upon the name of the prophet Malachi have been suggested. The messenger-prophet in Isaiah, and Elijah and John the Baptist, have been suggested also (cf. Isa. 40:3-5; Mal. 4:5).

What is to be made of this? Who is my messenger? One who is to prepare the way of the Lord is presented in Isaiah 40:3-5; he may be identified as the Elijah of Malachi 4:5. The gospel writers affirm that John the Baptist is the messenger of Isaiah and the Elijah of Malachi (cf. Matt. 3:1-3; Mark 1:3; Luke 3:4). John the Baptist identified himself as the voice in the wilderness (cf. Isa. 40:3-5; Jno. 1:19-23). The angel of the Lord declared to Zacharias, the father of John the Baptist, that John would go before the Lord in the spirit and power of Elijah (cf. Luke 1:17, 76). The language used here in the gospel according to Luke appears to be based on Isaiah 40:3-5 and Malachi 4:5. Jesus identified John the Baptist as the one who fulfilled the prophecy of Malachi (cf. Matt. 11:10; Luke 7:26-28). He declared that John was the Elijah that should come (cf. Matt. 11:14). Again, when the disciples inquired about the coming of Elijah, the answer of Jesus was understood to be a reference to John the Baptist (cf. Matt. 17:12f). It should be reiterated that Malachi did not give the name of a person who would be the messenger. It is evident, however, that the providence of the Lord ordered the life of John the Baptist so as to fulfill the prophecies of Isaiah and Malachi.

The purpose of the coming of this messenger is to prepare the way before the Lord. The terminology which is used would be clear to an oriental audience. It was the custom for messengers or runners to be dispatched to towns and villages to announce the coming of kings and other dignataries who would be passing by. This enabled the people to have due notice thereof and to govern themselves accordingly. The preparation sometimes required the removal of rocks, filling holes, and the clearing of forests. Every impediment in the way of travel was to be removed. Care was exercised to see that the reception with which the coming one met was in accord with the dignity of his person and his office. This kind of preparation is emphasized by the prophet Isaiah (cf. 40:3-5; 57:14; 62:10). Although no details are given by Malachi regarding the work of the messenger who is to come, the importance of his work is evident because of the person for whom he is to make preparation. The ministry of John the Baptist tells the story of the work of the messenger who prepared the way for the coming one. It was moral and spiritual in its nature. It involved the road that leads to God and permits him to come to his own. John preached repentance, presented the redeemer, pled for righteousness, and provided for a reckoning (cf. Matt. 3:1-12).

The Messenger of the Covenant Is the Lord Himself (3:1b)

3:1b And suddenly the Lord whom you are seeking will proceed to come unto his temple, even the messenger of the covenant whom you are desiring, behold he comes, says Yahweh of hosts.

Even though a messenger is sent to prepare the way for the coming of this exalted one, the time of his appearing is not given. He is described as coming suddenly; he is the Lord whom they were seeking, and he will come unto his temple.

The term translated Lord (*adon*), which may signify master or owner, should not be regarded as a synonym or a substitute for Yahweh in this context. Translations indicate this by writing it with only one capital letter, whereas the substitute for Yahweh is written LORD. Here the prophet presents God in the role of his ownership of and Lordship over all things, including the temple. His appearance in *his* temple must be associated with the quest of the people. It is related to 2:17 by some interpreters.

His coming, therefore, is to meet the challenge of the cynics and to do something about entrenched evil that is in the world. This evidently is true, but there is more. It suggests that the one who comes has been the object of the quest of some from the morning of time. He has spoken through angels, prophets, psalmists, and other personalities. Natural phenomena and his providences declare his glory. His coming is to his temple, the place where he had manifested himself in veiled forms and meaningful symbols. It was the place where people assembled for worship, but their worship had become a vain and condemned practice (cf. Mal. 2:11; Isa. 1:11ff.; 56:7; Jer. 7:11). The messenger's appearance will be awesome, for Habakkuk says, "But the Lord is in his holy temple; let all the earth keep silence before him" (cf. Hab. 2:20).

He is further described by the words " 'even the messenger of the covenant whom you are desiring, behold, he comes,' says Yahweh of hosts." The Hebrew word given in this translation as "even" is either a demonstrative adverb or a conjunction. It is translated in the KJV. The translation is significant in the interpretation of the terms "my messenger," "the Lord," and "the messenger of the covenant." Some regard all three terms to be a reference to one person. Others consider them to be a designation of at least two people, the last two having reference to the Lord. The translation given in the KJV and that of the writer sees the Lord and the messenger of the covenant as one and the same. Dentan regarded the messenger of the covenant to be an angel.[1] Smith declared that the significance of the term cannot be determined.[2] Cashdan quoted Kimchi and Metsudath David who identified this messenger as Elijah.[3] The guardian angel of the Jewish community (cf. Zech. 1:12; 3:1; Dan. 10:5; 12:1), and the angel of the covenant with Baal Berith have been suggested.[4] He is the messenger of the covenant whose pre-incarnate manifestations are seen on numerous occasions, including covental relationships (cf. Gen. 16:7; Ex. 3:2f.; 23:20-23; Judg. 6:11ff.; 13:21-22). The covenant that was made at Sinai in which Yahweh chose the nation of Israel and became their God is the one to which the prophets refer. They never mention the covenant with Abraham. As in the case of the messenger who was sent to prepare the way for the

[1] R. C. Dentan, "The Book of Malachi," p. 1137.

[2] J. M. P. Smith, Ward and Bewer, *A Critical and Exegetical Commentary on the Book of Malachi*, p. 63.

[3] Cashdan, "Malachi," p. 349.

[4] Matthews, "Haggai, Malachi," p. 29.

coming of the Lord, the authority of the New Testament is significant in identifying the messenger of the covenant (cf. Heb. 8:7-11 and Jer. 31:31-34; Heb. 12:24; 13:20; Matt. 26:28). Thus the one presented in Malachi who is called the messenger of the covenant is none other than the Lord. This conclusion is supported by the fact that if the work of the messenger of the covenant is distinct from that of the Lord, it is not stated. The context which presents the one in the role of judgment and cleansing declares him to be the Lord (cf. 3:5-6).

BY SEVERE PURGING (3:2-6)

Here the prophet magnifies the fact that love can be severe. It has to do with discipline that is designed to bless. This aspect of divine love often is overlooked, and many who experience it are unprepared to accept it when it comes.

Creating Fear (3:2-3a)

3:2 But who will be able to go on abiding in the day of his coming? And who is the one keeping on standing when he appears? because he is like fire of a refiner and like soap of a fuller,

3a for he will sit as a refiner and purifier of silver . . . .

The questions which are asked indicate a visitation of severe judgment by the Lord when he comes to his temple. It will reveal the impurity and helplessness of all who are brought into his presence (cf. Isa. 33:14; Ezek. 22:14; Ps. 1:5). This is the old theme of Amos, Joel, and Zephaniah in their visions and declarations concerning the severity of the day of Yahweh (Amos 5:18-20; Joel 2:11; Zeph 1:15). Thus Malachi says it will be an awesome day, one of terror and dread. He does not say there will be no survivors, but he raises questions that indicate that some will not be able to endure the ordeal.

"Because he is like fire of a refiner and like soap of a fuller." The prophet employs the work and skills of the two ancient and familiar trades of refining metals and washing clothes to reveal that the process is not designed for total destruction. It will be for the purpose of the refinement and cleansing of his own. The dross will be burned out and the filth washed away. These are the things which have made the offerings and worship unacceptable. The peoples' lives are a contradiction of Yahweh's expectation and a stumbling block before sinners (2:5-9). It will be even as the Lord says through Zechariah:

And I will put this third into the fire, and refine them as one refines silver, and test them as gold is tested. They will call on my name, and I will answer them. I will say, "They are my people;" and they will say, "The Lord is my God." (cf. (Zech. 13:9; cf. also Isa. 1:21-27; 4:2-7; Jer. 9:7; Prov. 3:11-12; Hosea 2:14ff.; Matt. 3:10-12; I Cor. 3:13-15).

"And he will sit as a refiner and purifier of silver" carrying out the process with precision and care (cf. Job 23:10; Prov. 17:3; Isa. 48:9-11; 1 Pet. 1:7). The Lord exercises a watchful eye, pours in his tears of love, and performs the work with a steady hand. The fires are not permitted to become too hot nor is the process left incomplete. This great truth is illustrated by Bishop in a quotation from Neil:

. . . We see the jeweller sitting over the melting pot, while he blows the flame to a greater heat. . . the refiner looks into the open furnace or pot and knows that the process of purifying is complete, and the dross all burnt away, when he can see his own image plainly reflected in the molten metal.[1]

Involving the Sons of Levi (3:3b-4)

3:3b . . . and he will purify the sons of Levi, and refine them as gold and silver; and they shall be to Yahweh offerers of offerings in righteousness.

4 Then shall be pleasant to Yahweh the offering of Judah and Jerusalem, as in the days of old, even as in ancient years.

This is the first reference in the above text to people who will be involved in the chastening of the Lord. The purification of

---

[1]Eric F. F. Bishop, *Prophets of Palestine* (London: Lutterworth Press, 1962), p. 259.

the sons of Levi is because of their failure to bring offerings to Yahweh in righteousness. They will be purged of unbelief, irreverence, impurity, and corrupt teaching (cf. 1:2; 2:9; Isa. 4:3-6; Job 28:1; Jer. 6:27-30). This judgment upon the defunct spiritual leaders who were called of God, endowed, and made accountable stewards is not without precedent (cf. Lev. 10:1ff.; 1 Sam. 2:27f.; Jonah 1:1ff.) This picture of the purging of the Lord's people is proclaimed by another messenger of the Lord:

> For the time has come for the judgment to begin with the household of God; and if it begins with us, what will be the end of those who do not obey the gospel of God? And "If the righteous man is scarcely saved, where will the impious and sinner appear?" (I Peter 4:17)

When the work of purging, like that of straining wine (cf. Isa. 25:6) and of the refining of precious metals (cf. Ps. 66:10) has been done, then shall the offering of Judah and Jerusalem be pleasing to Yahweh. This will come to pass when the fountainhead of religious leadership is purified and the people at large become pleasing to him. Then offerings will be presented by clean hands and motivated by the love and devotion of pure hearts (cf. Ps. 24:4). The psalmist prays for the Lord to create in him a clean heart and to renew within him a right spirit. Afterwards he declares, "Then wilt thou delight in the sacrifices of righteousness, in burnt offering and whole burnt offering; then will they offer bullocks upon thine altar" (cf. 51:10, 19).

This purging which Malachi emphasizes will take place as in the days of old, and as in ancient years. The interpreter is at a loss to know just what period in Israel's history may be in the mind of the prophet in the expression "in the days of old." It may be a reference to the "good old days" that are idealized and made more acceptable because of their antiquity. It could be that the prophet, looking upon the corruption and hypocrisy of his time, considers any previous day to be better than his (cf. 2:2-3). He could be speaking of the early days in the wilderness when the sacrifices and worship offered by the people could have been idealized as more pleasing to God (cf. Isa. 63:9; Hos. 2:15; Jer. 2:2-3, 13). It may be a reference to the time of Samuel or to the early days of Solomon's reign when the temple was first completed (cf. 1 Sam. 7:3ff.; 1 Kings 8).

Condemning Specific Sins (3:5)

3:5 And I will draw near unto you for judgment, and I will be a swift witness against the sorcerers, against the adulterers, and against the false swearers, and against those who oppress the wage earner with respect to his wages, the widow and the orphan, against those who push aside the foreigner, and they do not reverence me, says Yahweh of hosts.

"And I will draw near to you for judgment" is a message to the people in general. If they had rejoiced when the religious leadership was arraigned and condemned, they need to know that their day is at hand. The summary of their sin is without a superfluous word. It is a proclamation that is clear and unmistakable. The whole sordid picture is splashed on the canvas with one stroke of the brush. When the voice of the prophet dies away, the thunders of the eighth century prophets who also preached against these sins can be heard in the background. The prophets could do no other, because Yahweh is in the conflict for social justice. His concern is perennial, and his way must prevail.

This is the only time the word "judgment" is used in the book of Malachi, although the concept of it appears all the way through it. Here, as he does so often, Yahweh assumes the role of judge and witness as he opens his solemn assize. As a witness he will be swift and ready to tell all that he knows about the defendants under the highest oath, and it will be the truth. None of the accused will be able to refute the word of the witness. As judge he will confront all who had accused him of being no judge at all (cf. 2:17). His judgment will be true and fair, and the sentence will be passed because the judge of all the earth will do right (cf. Gen. 19:25). The proclamation of judgment was prominent among Malachi's predecessors. The foundation of all of their preaching was based on Exodus 34:6-7. The lovingkindness, patience, and forgiveness of God are magnified. But his judgment will inevitably fall upon all who persist in their sin. This judgment will demonstrate the sovereignty of God, the folly of sin, and the wisdom of righteousness.

The sins which are to be judged relate to the religious and social practices of the people. They are the kinds of things that can thrive among any people when the worship of God and his way are repudiated. It is significant that other prophets condemn the sins which are listed in Malachi 3:5. A proclamation of Jeremiah declares:

Behold, you trust in deceptive words to no avail.
Will you steal, murder, commit adultery, swear
falsely, burn incense to Baal, and go after
other gods that you have not known,
and then come and stand before me in this
house, which is called by my name, and say,
"We are delivered!"—only to go on doing all
these abominations? (Jer. 7:8-10).

Amos, Hosea, and Micah also are heard (cf. Amos 8:5-6; Hos. 4:1-2; Mic. 3:11).

Sorcery, an effort to gain power through evil spirits, necromancy, witchcraft and related evils, was condemned in Israel (cf. Deut. 18:9-18). Sorcery was practiced in Egypt in the time of Moses (cf. Ex. 7:11), and Israel was commanded to put sorcerers to death (cf. Ex. 22:18; Lev. 20:27). Such practices were considered evil not only because they were a part of heathen worship and corruption, but they represented rebellion against God and the message which he proclaimed through his prophets (cf. Jer. 27:9). A classic example of this heathen art is found in Saul's experience with the necromancer (cf. 1 Sam. 28:3ff.).

Adultery is characterized by many things. Idolatrous worship in Israel was considered to be spiritual adultery (cf. Hosea 1:2; 2:2ff.; Ezek. 16:15f.). Here, as in numerous other places in the Old Testament, it refers to moral corruption, including marital infidelity. The seventh commandment declares, "thou shall not commit adultery" (cf. Ex. 20:14). Idolatrous practices, emphasizing the sympathetic magic of the fertility cult, encouraged and protected adultery as a part of worship (cf. Amos 2:7). Contrary to the opinion of some interpreters, adultery was widespread in Israel (cf. Hosea 4:2, 14; 7:4; Jer. 29:23; Ezek. 22:11).

False swearing is forbidden as a violation of God's law (cf.

Ex. 20:16; 23:1, 7; Prov. 19:5). The psalmist complains about unrighteous witnesses confronting him (cf. 35:11), and he declares his hatred of false ways (cf. 119:104).

A word is sounded against those who oppress the wage earner with respect to his wages. The word of the Lord through the prophet Amos condemns Israel—"because they sell the righteous for silver, and the needy for a pair of shoes—they that trample the head of the poor into the dust of the earth. . . ." (2:6-7). There are other strong pronouncements against this corruption that leave no comfort for the guilty (cf. Deut. 15:7-18; 24:14-15; Isa. 5:8; Micah 2:1-2). It may be declared that if one loves God, he cannot mistreat and trample upon his fellowman. Withholding of wages is condemned as failure to pay what one promises, but it also should include what one ought to have been promised and paid as a just wage.

Those who oppress widows and orphans are sharply condemned. Fearful words are written in the Scriptures which declare the judgment of the Almighty against this sin (cf. Ex. 22:22-24; Deut. 24:14b; Ps. 68:6; 103:6). Among a long list of imperatives Isaiah commands, "defend the fatherless, plead for the widow" (cf. 1:17).

Condemnation is sounded against those who push aside the foreigner. The concern expressed in the Scriptures in behalf of the sojourner involves his full protection. He is not to be forced to labor on the Sabbath day (cf. Ex. 23:12); he is to be treated by his master as if he were born to him and to be loved by him (cf. Lev. 19:34). The foreigner was to be given gleaning privileges in the fields, special considerations in a portion of the tithe, and protection in the courts (cf. Lev. 23:22; Deut. 14:29; 24:17; 27:19).

The parent of all of the sins described above is revealed and condemned in the words, " 'and they do not fear me,' says Yahweh of hosts." The word "fear" is to be understood as reverence or godly awe. The rebellion of the wicked people reveals that they do not reverence God (cf. Ps. 36:1). When godly awe has no place in one's life, one is liable to become the victim of all kinds of evil passions and lusts (cf. Rom. 1:18ff.; 3:18). There is a need to be controlled by a humble, reverent recognition of God as God, and the realization of the wretchedness and wickedness of man in his sight. "The fear of the Lord is the beginning of knowledge . . ." (cf. Prov. 1:7; Job 28:28). God is to be served or worshipped in fear (cf. Ps. 2:11; 4:7). "In the fear of the Lord one has strong confidence . . . and a fountain of life" (cf. Prov. 14:26-27). Reverence for God will lead to faith in him and obedience to his commands (Gen. 22:12; Ex. 14:31). To experience the forgiveness of God will lead one to reverence him (cf. Ps. 130:4). It is God's desire that we may obey his words and learn to reverence him all the days of our lives (cf. Deut. 4:10). The writer of the book of Ecclesiastes declares, "The end of the matter; all has been heard. Fear God, and keep his commandments; for this is the whole duty of man" (12:13).

Sparing a Remnant (3:6)

3:6 For I Yahweh, do not change; therefore you, O sons of Jacob are not consumed.

At least one interpreter dismissed this verse with two disparaging sentences. On account of the fact that there does not appear to be any justifiable reason for rejecting the above translation as it is given, an effort will be made to interpret it. There is no support for the view that God is virtually retracting the condemnation of the sins which are clearly set forth in verse 5. Nor does it mean that no punishment will be meted out. What it does mean is that mercy will be mingled with judgment (cf. Isa. 48:9-11). The people will not be consumed or destroyed. These facts are justified on the basis of the unchanging character of God. He is the same yesterday and today and forever (cf. Heb. 13:8). On the one hand, he is a God of mercy, on the other, he is a God of justice. The hope for the preservation of the people is based on their repentance and God's readiness to forgive. These facts are revealed and experienced throughout Israel's history. They are confirmed in God's dealings with Israel in the wilderness, the period of the Judges, the stormy eighth and seventh centuries, and the restoration from exile. All the prophets declare God's judgment against sin, but they hold out hope for penitent sinners.

This verse is taken to mean that God's moral character remains unchanged. This is a significant teaching in the Old Testament (cf. Ps. 90:1-2; 102:26ff.; Deut. 33:27). Hosea declares that it is because God is God, and not man, that he will not make a total end of his people (cf. 11:8-9). There are accounts of God's repentance, understood sometimes as having compassion. Sometimes as turning away from something which it seemed that he had purposed to do (cf. Gen. 6:6; 1 Sam. 15:29; Joel 2:13; Jonah 3:10). Repentance of evil as it is used with God is a judgment or a calamity, not moral evil or sin. God is altogether righteous and in him is no sin at all. In instances such as Numbers 23:19 and Psalm 110:4, it is declared that God will not repent. The fact that he is said to repent and that he will not repent should not be considered as contradictions. The meaning of the term must be understood in the context where it is found. When man's sin is taken into account, if he repents and turns from it, God is said to repent and to turn from the judgment which he had purposed to visit upon the impenitent (cf. Jonah 3:5-10). It is in the light of these facts that Malachi 3:6 must be understood and interpreted. It is because of God's longsuffering, and his hope that repentance will come that the people are consumed (cf. 3:7; Ex. 34:6-7; Jer. 30:11; Ezek. 33:11). The unchanging one is consistent in his character. What he is and what he does are one and the same. It may be said that he always forgives the penitent and punishes the impenitent. He does not change. Mays said:

> Yahweh's refusal to destroy Israel is no concession to their sin, no curtailment of discipline; but it is a declaration that his relationship in history with Israel shall not end because of their sin and his wrath.[1]

It should be recalled that Yahweh threatened to destroy all mankind in the time of the flood. He found a righteous remnant and spared them (cf. Gen. 6:5-8). His longsuffering and covenant love prevailed again when he threatened to destroy all but one in Israel (cf. Ex. 32:7-14).

---

[1] James Luther Mays, *Hosea: A Commentary* (Philadelphia: Westminster Press, 1969), p. 158.

VII. Divine Love Demands Obedience

INVOLVING ORDINANCES LONG DISOBEYED (3:7a)

3:7a From the days of your fathers you have turned aside from my statutes, and have not kept them.

Here is a declaration of perpetual backsliding, a turning away from known duty to other ways which the people desired, dating back to ancient days. Although the exact time of the beginning point is not stated, it would appear to extend as far back as the patriarchs (cf. Isa. 48:27; Jer. 3:6; 22; 7:25-26; 16:11-12; Hos. 10:9).

The sin with which they are charged involves failure to observe certain enactments or statutes which were given by the Lord as a part of covenant responsibility. These enactments pertained to their total life. Social, economic, political, and religious responsibilities are specifically declared. They were understood to be the revealed will of God which had been accepted (cf. Ex. 19:8; 24:3). The fact that infractions involving these laws were to meet with judgment also was known. Violators, therefore, were without excuse. There is a marked contrast in their failures and God's steadfast love in keeping his promises to them (cf. Ex. 34:6).

THE CALL TO RETURN (3:7b)

3:7b "Return unto me for I am determined to return unto you," says Yahweh of hosts.

This is a positive command which is expressed by the special form of the imperative. It has the tone of strong entreaty, emphasizing the importance and urgency of the plea. It is a call to repentance, which includes turning from evil and turning to God. It is more than ritual observances and outward forms (cf. Amos 5:4-5). People who turned away from God's commands also rejected his ways.

The entreaty to come back to God is in the language of a compassionate father who longed for his son to be with him and to be obedient to him. The appeal is made to the people to return on the basis of their having turned away from God in the free exercise of their choice. It must be their will to come back if the decision is made. God's passionate concern is reflected in the language, "For I am determined to return unto you." The meaning here is, "if you will repent of your sin, I will repent of my judgment." It expresses that fact that God has set himself to remove every thing that may stand in the way of reconciling and reclaiming his wayward children short of overriding their wills, a thing that he cannot do if man is to be man and if obedience is to be obedience. But the experience of God's grace depends on the proper attitude of the would-be recipients.

Malachi's predecessors often called to the wayward people to return to God. Isaiah entreats for God when he says, "Come now, let us reason together . . . ." (cf. 1:18). Jeremiah pleads, "Return, O faithless sons. . ." (cf. 3:22), and Hosea says, "Come, let us return to the Lord. . ." (cf. 6:1). Ezekiel entreats, ". . . turn back, turn back from your evil ways; for why will you die, O house of Israel?" (33:11).

THE CALL TO RETURN IS SPURNED (3:7c)

3:7c But you say, "Wherein shall we return?"
The call to repent is met with the same insolent reply which
prevails throughout this discourse when the people are confronted with their sin. It is as if they were saying, "Repent? In
what way do we need to repent? Come now and tell us." This is
an evidence of their obstinate nature, self-righteousness, declaration of innocence, and sullen spirit. It is an artful device to
evade responsibility and an unwillingness to face the issues (cf.
Micah 6:6-7).

OBEDIENCE INVOLVES THE TITHE (3:8)

**3:8 Will a man rob God? Yet you are going on robbing me.
But you say, "Wherein have we robbed you?" In the
tithes and offerings.**
The prophet replies with a question which expects a negative
answer, thereby magnifying the heinous offense of which his
people are guilty. It is as if he were saying, "A man may
defraud or rob his neighbor, or even his father or mother; but
surely he would not rob God" (cf. Lev. 19:13; Prov. 28:24). In
spite of the fact that the charge is without reason, the prophet
asserts that it is true. What is more, it is not something that
has happened occasionally and in isolated cases among the less
fortunate. It is a continuous, never ending practice of all the
people. "Wherein have we robbed you?" Thus the charge, one of
the most serious that the prophet had made, met with their
same characteristic, cynical response. They virtually say,
"Robbing God? That is ridiculous. How could we be robbing
God and of what?"
The question does not catch the prophet unprepared or afraid
to answer. The robbing of which the nation is guilty is "in the
tithes and the offerings" which they are commanded to pay into
the treasury of the temple for the support of the ministry, the
relief of the poor, and every other work of God. The use of the
definite article suggests that the possessions which the people

were commanded to bring were preferred items upon which prior claims had been made.

The tithe is one-tenth of the income. It is the Lord's by reason of his having set it apart for his use (cf. Lev. 27:30; Num. 18:21; Deut. 14:22f.). It is declared to be holy, set aside, and reserved for the Lord's use. The paying of the tithe was an ancient practice in Israel and among other people as well. It was known to Abraham and Jacob and apparently observed by them (cf. Gen. 14:18-20; 28:18-22). There are many accounts in the Old Testament which emphasize the responsibility of tithing. There appear to be some regulations concerning the budgeting and use of the tithe. It is rather clear that a tenth of the income of the people was to be given to the Lord for the support of the priests and Levites and to meet other needs in the Lord's work. The word for offering which is used here is associated with the heave offering in numerous places in the Old Testament (cf. Ex. 30:14; Num. 15:19-21; Deut. 12:6, 11, 17). Offerings were set apart for the priests and Levites, materials for the tabernacle, priestly garments, and for temple use (cf. Lev. 7:14; Num. 5:9; Ex. 25:2-3; 35:5ff.; Ezra 8:25). Many other offerings are specified which the people gave. Like all other gifts, they were things that cost the people something. They were not attained through suppers and sales in the name of the temple. No amount of the offering is specified because they were free will gifts.

No defense against the charge of robbing God is offered by the people. But one may surmise that they thought, "as long as we have poor harvests, we have no other choice. God is responsible for drought, insects, and crop failure. It will not be possible for us to do more as long as these things persist." When expenses increase without any increase in income, the Lord's cause is the first to suffer. That is as true today as in Malachi's day. The Lord's cause is more remote and less exacting than life's material demands such as groceries, clothing, rent, and automobiles. The paying of tithes and offerings is not determined by any amount of income, nor will the high cost of living, low income, and hardships dry up the fountains of generosity. Faith and loyalty will decide the issue. Tithe tides are determined by the winds of religious zeal, devotion to God, and gratitude for his blessings.

All questions, objections, and disobedience regarding tithes and offerings did not die with Malachi's generation. This kind of talk has a familiar ring in the church today. Calkins called attention to the fact that:

It is said that nowadays the work and support of a church is borne by one-third of its congregation; another third looks on; and the remaining third does not know what it is all about. We need in our day, as truly as Malachi urged the need of his day, a revival of interest upon the laity as a whole in the corporate life of the Church. Until the day of that revival comes, Zion will continue to languish.[1]

The robbing of God has not ceased in a Christian era when gifts should be more generous and more freely given. The apostle Paul admonishes:

Each one must do as he has made up his mind, not reluctantly or under compulsion, for God loves a cheerful giver. And God is able to provide you with every blessing in abundance, so that you may always have enough of everything and may provide in abundance for every good work. As it is written, "He scatters abroad, he gives to the poor; his righteousness endures for ever." (II Cor. 9:7-9).

THE CURSE OF DISOBEDIENCE (3:9)

3:9 With the curse are you being cursed, for me you keep on robbing, the whole nation of you.

These words tell of the judgment of God upon the guilty. It is visited by means of drought, poor crops, plagues of locusts, and a blight or mildew (cf. 3:11; Hab. 3:17; Hag. 1:5, 9-11). Many spiritual blessings were not experienced because there was no room for them. The first curse of which there is any record in the Bible is that which is pronounced upon the serpent (cf. Gen. 3:14). A detailed account of the visitation of the curse upon the disobedient is given in Deuteronomy 28:15-68 (cf. Lev. 26:14-45; Hag. 1:5f.; Zech. 5:1-4).

[1]Raymond Calkins, *The Modern Message of the Minor Prophets*, p. 140.

The text of Malachi declares that the curse which is pronounced upon and hangs over the disobedient will not be removed until its cause is removed, in this instance the robbing of God. Syntax, which has to do with the arrangement of words in a sentence, puts the emphasis on the pronoun "me" as a means of magnifying the enormity and hatefulness of the sin of the people. It is not the priests and the Levites; it is not the temple, or its altars; it is not the government; it is God who is being robbed. The concern of God in this arraignment and charge is not for himself or his needs. "The earth is the Lord's and the fulness thereof; the world, and those who dwell therein" (cf. Ps. 24:1). In another testimony through the psalmist, the Lord says, "For every beast of the forest is mine, and the cattle upon a thousand hills. If I were hungry, I would not tell you; for the world and all that is in it is mine" (cf. Ps. 50:10, 12). It is to be concluded, however, that God expects and demands that which he has made holy for his own service (cf. Lev. 27:30-33; Num. 18:21-31). Smith concludes:

> If tempted to see in this a legal spirit, let us remember that the neglect to pay tithes was due to a religious cause, unbelief in God, and that return to belief in Him could not be shown in a more practical way than by paying tithes. This is not prophecy subject to the Law, but prophecy employing the means and vehicles of grace with which the Law then provided the people. [1]

THE BLESSINGS OF OBEDIENCE (3:10-12)

3:10 "Bring the full tithe into the storehouse, that there may be food in my house; and put me to the test now by this (means)," says Yahweh of hosts, "if I will not continually open the windows of the heavens, and pour down to you a blessing in full measure.

11 And I will rebuke for you the devourer, and he will not destroy the fruits of your soil; and your vine in the field shall not fail to bear," says Yahweh of hosts.

[1] George Adam Smith, *The Book of the Twelve Prophets,* p. 360.

12 "Then all the nations shall abundantly bless you, because you, even you, will be a delightful land," says Yahweh of hosts.

The call to bring the full tithes is an imperative, a positive command. The emphasis is strong, and it demands all of the tithe. This may be an indication that some people had brought part of it, but the full force of the command was not obeyed. The place to pay the tithe is the storehouse. This constitutes the treasury of the temple (cf. 1 Kings 7:51; Neh. 10:38-39; 13:12-13). The purpose for bringing the tithe is to provide the needs of God's house. The words "meat" or "food" indicate physical needs.

" '. . . and put me to the test now by this (means),' says Yahweh of hosts," is unique terminology. It is expected that God will test the faith and devotion of his own. It is declared that God proved, tested, literally, "smelled out" Abraham (cf. Gen. 22:1). Satan sometimes desires to test us (cf. Luke 22:31). When Satan was tempting Jesus, it is declared that "Jesus said to him, 'Again it is written, you shall not tempt the Lord your God' " (cf. Matt. 4:7). This is a quotation from Deuteronomy 6:16. The meaning of the mandate is that one is not to act in a presumptuous manner. He is not to be foolish.

The Lord's challenge for people to test him is in answer to the charge in 2:17. The bringing of the tithe is made a test regarding God's faithfulness and justice. He had been accused of failing to bless, either because he delighted in people who did evil, or he was unjust. The declaration is that the failure was theirs and not his. The challenge to test him is for the purpose of proving his ability and his willingness to prove himself. The term is sometimes used of God's trying or testing persons (cf. Ps. 66:10; Job 23:10; Zech. 13:9). Here the great God of heaven challenges frail, failing people to put him to the test (cf. Gen. 18:22ff.; Judges 6:36f.; Isa. 7:10).

"If I will not continually open the windows of the heavens and pour down to you a blessing in full measure" is God's declaration of intent. The guarantee is from God himself. It will be given through the open windows of the heavens. The assurance is that the blessing will be repeatedly given in full measure. The opening of the windows of the heavens suggests the giving of the necessary rain and favorable seasons for fruitful harvests. It is not an exact parallel to the miracle of the wilderness (cf. Ex. 16:4ff.), but it is the work of God who provides for his own. If the tithes and offerings are brought regularly to prove God, the rains will come in season and so will the harvests. Then the flood gates will be opened and the showers of blessing will come down (cf. Deut. 28:12-13; 2 Kings 7:2; Ezek. 34:25-31).

The blessing promised by the Lord is one of fulness. There will be no way to measure it. The supply will be beyond the demand. The barns will be too small for the harvests (cf. 2 Chron. 31:4-10; Luke 12:16-18). The plowman will catch up with the reaper (cf. Amos 9:13).

This imperative and the ensuing promise of plenty create serious problems for the interpreter. How are these things to be understood? Shall one pay his tithe and bring some offerings and expect to receive back more than he gave? This is a vending machine concept, a dollar for dollar equation. The mind of the Hebrews must be sought as an aid in understanding the promise. On account of the limited knowledge of life beyond death, strong emphasis was placed on the blessings to be received here and now. There is nothing inconsistent in this concept in the Old Testament era.

Kennedy observed that the prophet Joel "places emphasis on the Lord's concern for the whole life of the people." He further states that "no equation is drawn between the degree of faithfulness to God and the measure of material prosperity, for none is possible. But neither is separation assumed between physical disaster and moral disintegration, for frequently the two are inter-related . . . on the basis of his own goodness and grace, he (the Lord) announced forgiveness and abundant favors to the penitent (2:12-14, 18-19)."[1]

When the above considerations are ignored, tithing becomes a means of having unlimited financial returns on the limited investment which people make in the Lord's work. It has been regarded as God's way of offering a payoff, a safe investment

[1] J. Hardee Kennedy, "Joel," *The Broadman Bible commentary*, ed. by Clifton J. Allen, Vol. VII (Nashville: Broadman Press, 1972), p. 66.

with a guaranteed return, in order to get the needed funds for his cause. This is to inject a mercenary motive in spiritual worship and service. Sensitive souls look for a better way.

When considering the relationship of the material to the spiritual in the Old Testament where the material sometimes appears to play a dominant role, it is helpful to bear in mind the theological presuppositions of the Old Testament writers. The Deuteronomic emphasis seeks to supply the answer both for this life and for life after death. Unimpeachable evidence which was believed to justify claims for righteousness was found in prosperity and blessing in this life (cf. Job, esp. 22:21-30). Job, although justified as a righteous man by the Lord, was condemned as a sinner by his contemporaries because of his suffering and material loss. This understanding of blessings and well-being in this world also must be interpreted in keeping with the belief that there was no advantage for the righteous over the wicked in their eternal abode. Rewards and punishments were not a part of their existence in Sheol.

Scott observed:

In later writings the *material* blessings of the 'Messianic age' are over-emphasized. But in essence they belong, like the hope of the Davidic family who would be a true vice-gerent of Yahweh, to the conception that God's final salvation is to be achieved *within* history. It will not be different in kind—from Yahweh's historic acts—his self-manifestation in the election, the deliverances and the judgments which his people had known. Rather, it will be but the completion of what he had begun—a consummation assured by Yahweh's sovereignty, but the consistency of his ethical will and the tireless goodness of his purpose.[1]

Finally, it must be said that altogether too much emphasis is placed on material blessings and comforts when the promises of God are considered. The text declares that the heavens will be opened and blessings without measure will be given. Verse 11 is the basis for the restricted emphasis on the blessings of the field. When the blessings of God are considered, is God to be considered so limited? What shall be said for the knowledge of God, justification from sin, and fellowship with him? All of

[1]Scott, *The Relevance of the Prophets,* pp. 156-57.

these are blessings from God. The command to bring the tithe was a call to give tangible evidence of repentance and faith. This proclamation and response illustrate the cooperation of law and grace in spiritual achievement. Tithing in itself cannot be regarded as a guarantee that all good things will be given to the tither. Not all sinners have it hard, and not all the righteous travel the high road of ease and success. God does not settle all his accounts, neither does he provide abundant harvests in October, either for the righteous or for the wicked. But when a life is surrendered to Yahweh, tithing is a by-product of that surrender, and such a life is blessed. Even suffering becomes an avenue of good (cf. Rom. 8:28). The one who gives and gives himself enjoys the blessing of being like God, because he is more like him when he gives than in any other way. In his discussion of this text, Maclaren said:

> This is the universal law, not always fulfilled in increase of outward goods, but in the better riches of communion and of larger possession in God himself. He suffers no man to be His creditor, but more than returns our gifts, as legends tell of some peasant who brought his king a poor tribute of fruits of his field, and went away from the presence-chamber with a jewel in his hand.[1]

Verse 11 is the continuation of the emphasis on the blessing. The Lord promises to take away the hindrances which are ever present plagues in the fields. Rebuke means to nullify or to drive away. The devourer is not identified, and there are several candidates for this work. Drought, locusts, hail, and mildew were the more common plagues that wrought havoc against the crops (cf. Joel 1:2-4; 2:18-27; Hag. 2:9-11). Any one of these things was likely to destroy the tender plants. It could reap the harvest while it was yet in the field. Sometimes one thing followed on the heels of another, bringing about total destruction (cf. Ex. 9:22ff.). It must be remembered that in Malachi's time there were no scientific means such as irrigation and pesticides to be employed to combat these destructive forces. The failing of the vine is literally a miscarriage in which the

[1]Alexander Maclaren, *The Books of Ezekiel, Daniel, and the Minor Prophets*, Expositions of Holy Scripture, Vol. VI (Grand Rapids: Wm. B. Eerdmans Publishing Co., 1959), p. 349.

fruit either dried up or rotted in the process of ripening (cf. Isa. 5:2; Hab. 3:17).

" 'Then all nations shall abundantly bless you; because you, even you, will be a delightsome land,' says Yahweh of hosts" (cf. Mal. 3:12; Deut. 28:1). This is the fruition of the promise of God to Abraham (cf. Gen. 12:1-3). It will be to the advantage of the nations to bless the people of God, for in so doing they will enter into the legacy of the blessings for themselves. This truth already had been declared.

God's blessings, which are without measure and come from unexpected sources and in uncalculated ways, will speak with authority. The nations that had cursed and scourged the people will turn around and bless them. This is the fulfillment of their greatest desires and hopes (cf. Isa. 60:3-14; 61:9; 62:1-4, 10-12). The promise of blessing to the obedient and of the plaudit of the nations had been proclaimed. Warning was given to those who turned away from God, and it was declared that they would be an object of scorn and contempt to all nations (cf. Deut. 28:1, 15; Ps. 31:19; I Kings 9:6-9).

An excellent summary of the New Testament teaching concerning stewardship, including tithing, is found in Frank Stagg's *New Testament Theology*, pp. 285-293.

VIII. Divine Love Expressed in Righteous Judgment

3:13 "Your words have been stout against me," says Yahweh. "But you say, 'What have we said against you?'

14 You have said, 'It is vain to serve God; and what profit do we get from keeping his charge, or that we walk mournfully before Yahweh of hosts?

15 And now we are blessing the proud; also the workers of iniquity are built up; yea, they tempt God and continue to escape.' "

16a Thus those who feared God did speak with one another.

At this point in the text the judgement draws nearer. It is judgment through love that seeks to redeem as long as there is any basis for appeal. This can be substantiated because God is not a capricious judge, and he is not willing that any man should perish, but that all should come to repentance (cf. 2 Peter 3:9).

These two facts provide a canopy for rebellious sinners on the one hand, and believers who have become critical of the Lord on the other. Both of these groups are dealt with in Malachi. These cynical and strong words had come from critical believers (cf. 2:17; 3:5; Job 21:14-15). It is possible that a partial reason for the attitude thus manifested was because of their sufferings and hardships. It must not be overlooked, however, that they were following the pattern of skeptical murmuring which marked the footsteps of some of their forefathers (cf. Ex. 16:2ff.). The context indicates that the people were reasoning back and forth (gossiping) among themselves. Their words did not please the Lord, and he rebuked them. The response which they made to the rebuke of the Lord is in the same fitful manner that is like an old song.

Their stout words are vocalized by the prophet's declaration, "You have said it is vain to serve God." This is the language of selfishness, arrogance, self-pity, and pessimism. The word vain suggests that which is foolish, insignificant, fruitless, or unprofitable (cf. Jer. 2:25, 30; 18:12; Ps. 127:1-2). God may be served in worship and in works (cf. Ex. 12:25ff.; Josh. 22:27).

"And what profit do we get from keeping his charge, or that we walk mournfully before Yahweh of hosts?" (cf. Mal. 3:14; Job 21:14-15). The question which is raised is a further emphasis on the vanity of serving God. It is the language of one who sits in the seat of the scornful (cf. Ps. 1:1). Frustrated, selfish believers often magnify what they do not have while closing their eyes to their rich heritage (cf. Luke 15:29-31). They reason that they have been faithful to the Lord and his church. Their tithes and offerings have been brought, and they have sought to live above reproach in the world.

The people ask, "What good has been derived from all of this devotion to God?" They judge it to be an empty, profitless endeavor. They boast of serving God and keeping his charge in such a way as to suggest that nothing was lacking in their devotion to him. The charge of the Lord has reference to his commandments and statutes. The idea of keeping suggests custodial duties. It also means a way of life that conforms to

God's requirements. Care had been exercised in walking in penitence, marked by fasting, weeping, and mourning. The first meaning of the word "mourning" is "black." It is used with reference to the color of the skin, the tents of the nomads, and the apparel of people in sorrow. It is the latter use that is employed in the text before us (cf. Job 5:11; Ps. 35:14; Jer. 14:2). In all probability the people were speaking of their observance of the special times of fasting which were instituted in Babylon (cf. Zech. 8:3ff.). They were not satisfied with the way the Deuteronomic formula was working. According to it, the righteous are blessed and the wicked are cursed. It was not working out in their favor. In fact, it appeared to be reversed since they considered that they had been true to God in all things. Bright has observed:

So always do men speak who would make God the servant of their small concerns, an instrument at their disposal, a sort of divine insurance against loss or damage. Such men will always be disappointed in God. For they do not know that God is not at all at their service but quite the other way around, is summoning them to the service of his Kingdom.[1]

The root meaning of the word translated "proud" in verse 15 is "to boil over." In reference to attitude it signifies insolence, fierceness, or arrogance. When these terms are associated with sin, they indicate that which is presumptuous, purposely planned, and carried out with a high hand (cf. Deut. 1:43; Ex. 21:14; Neh. 9:16). It is such people who are congratulated. It was not considered that pride goes before destruction, and that it is not of God (cf. 4:1; Prov. 16:18; 1 Jno. 2:16). It is not pride but humility that is the way of God for his people (cf. 2 Chron. 7:14; Mic. 6:8; Prov. 18:12; Isa. 57:15). The reasoning of the skeptical is that haughty, self-sufficient sinners are considered to have chosen the better part. They are built up. Everything they do is profitable, because prosperity is born of craftiness and wicked practices. Their ways are marked by lying, stealing, and corruption; but they are never sick or in trouble. They presume on God, tempting him. His judgment is challenged by their cynical unbelief and godless works. But

[1] John Bright, *The Kingdom of God*, p. 160.

nothing ever comes of it. Their sins never find them out (cf. Num. 32:23). They go on in their carefree way, while we are foolish enough to do right (cf. Jer. 12:16ff.).

Thus those who feared God did speak with one another. They took counsel of appearances and allowed doubt and pessimism to cloud the real issues. Their lamentation was like that of the psalmist when his feet trod a darksome path and his mood was one of discouragement (cf. Ps. 73:1ff.). The word "thus," translated "then" (KJV, ASV, RSV), has been among scholars the reason for not regarding the people who said, "it is vain to serve God," and the "Yahweh fearers" (vs. 16) as one and the same. Ancient authority (LXX and Syriac) gives support "for rendering the opening word of vs. 16 as 'thus' rather than 'then.' "[1] The arrogant and evil doers (vs. 15) are the godless ones about whom the doubters among God's servants are speaking (cf. vss. 13-14). These doubters are the same ones who were identified previously (cf. 2:17).

A significant and striking contrast to this spirit is provided by another prophet in his affirmation of faith:
Though the fig trees do not blossom,
nor fruit be on the vines,
the produce of the olive fail
and the fields yield no food,
the flock be cut off from the fold
and there be no herd in the stalls,
yet I will rejoice in the Lord,
I will joy in the God of my salvation.
God, the Lord, is my strength;
he makes my feet like hinds' *feet*,
he makes me tread upon my high places. (Hab. 3:17-19).

REMEMBERED BY YAHWEH AS HIS OWN POSSESSION (3:16b-17)

3:16b Then Yahweh proceeded to take heed and to hear, and a book of remembrance was written before him

[1]Bennett, "Malachi," p. 391.

> concerning those who feared Yahweh and thought on
> his name.
>
> 17   "And they shall be mine," says Yahweh of hosts, "a
> special possession in the day which I am going on
> making, and I will have compassion upon them, just
> as a man has compassion upon his son, the one who
> keeps on serving him."

The opening words of the text are often applied to man. It is natural to think of God as always hearing. The psalmist speaks a sure word when he says, "He will not let your foot be moved, he who keeps you will not slumber. Behold he who keeps Israel will neither slumber nor sleep. The Lord is your keeper; the Lord is your shade on your right hand" (cf. Ps. 121:3-5). To heed is to hearken with a mind to obey. God heard what was said and responded to it in ways that are in keeping with his character, vindicating the righteous and visiting punishment upon the wicked. He moves according to his time schedule, and he acts to prove that there is a difference between the righteous and the wicked. He is a God of justice, and it shall be seen.

". . . and a book of remembrance was written before him. . . ." Man is commanded in the Scriptures to remember many things. These things include the Sabbath day and his past experiences of the blessings of God (cf. Ex. 20:8; Deut. 8:2f.). It is declared that the Persian king kept a "book of memorable deeds" involving the subjects of his kingdom (cf. Esther 6:1). The psalmist rejoiced because the righteous shall be had in everlasting remembrance (Ps. 112:6). It is declared that God remembered his covenant in the sufferings of his people and in other experiences (cf. Ex. 2:24; Ps. 106:44-46; Lev. 26:42-45). He vowed that he would remember the sins of his people no more (cf. Jer. 31:34). The Lord is called on to remember his promises and his covenant (cf. Ex. 32:13; Neh. 1:8-9). Nehemiah entreated God to remember him and his good deeds (cf. Neh. 13:14). It is said that God remembers the wickedness of the wicked (cf. Hos. 7:2; 8:13).

This book of remembrance in Malachi has a rich heritage and a great depth of meaning. It must be associated with the biblical concept of salvation and its ultimate fulfillment in an eternal fellowship with God. Moses associated those who were forgiven of their sin with a book in which their names were written (Ex. 32:30-35). This same concept is found in the book of Daniel with a strong emphasis on the resurrection from the dead (cf. 12:1-3). The psalmist refers to the book of life which contains the names of the righteous (cf. 69:28). He also speaks of a book with reference to his sorrows (cf. 56:8). Isaiah calls attention to a writing, perhaps a book, of the names of the holy ones (cf. 4:3). The book of life motif is continued in the New Testament. Jesus admonished his disciples to rejoice because their names were written in heaven (cf. Luke 10:20). Paul spoke of some fellow workers whose names were in the book of life (cf. Phil. 4:3). The same concept is found in the book of Revelation (cf. 3:5). Books, including the book of life, are associated with the great white throne judgment involving the works of those who are judged (Rev. 20:11-15).

"And they shall be mine" are the words of Yahweh as he claims those who feared him and thought on his name. The prince of the prophets magnifies this ownership when he says, "But now thus says the Lord, he who created you, O Jacob, he who formed you, O Israel: 'Fear not, for I have redeemed you; I have called you by name, you are mine' " (cf. Isa. 43:1). This is the heritage of every one who believes in God. He is God's chosen possession (cf. Ex. 19:5; Deut. 7:6; 1 Peter 2:9-10). This special possession will be claimed, made sure, and glorified in the day which God is going on making. It is on its way even now, and it shall be manifested in the full fruition of the day of Yahweh. It will be the coronation day when he shall be acclaimed Lord of Lords and King of kings. This is the language of eschatology. It will be a day of the working of God at which time he will show compassion toward his chosen possession and will visit punishment on the wicked. It will be the kind of compassion that a father shows toward an obedient son who goes on serving him (cf. 1:2; Ps. 103:13-14). The punishment will provide sufficient revelation and knowledge for those who insisted that they wanted God to "make speed and hasten his work" (cf. Isa. 5:19). It will be a lesson for those who declared that "everyone who does evil is good in the sight of the Lord, and he delights in them." This, they said, is true;

they asked, "Where is the God of justice?" (cf. Mal. 2:17). Those who have not considered the operation of his hands will see when he does his work, his strange work, and brings to pass his act, his strange act (cf. Isa. 5:12; 28:21).

APPROVAL AND ACCEPTANCE OF THE DISCRIMINATING SENTENCE OF JUDGMENT (3:18)

3:18 Then you shall return and distinguish between the righteous and the wicked, between the one who keeps on serving God and one who never serves him.

The above declaration is the answer to the complaint which was registered in 2:17 and 3:13-15. The advantages of being a child of God will be manifested. There will be a distinction made between the righteous and the wicked when the wheat and the tares are separated (cf. Gen. 18:25; Amos 5:15; Matt. 13:24-30). The word return may be translated "repent." If this is the meaning, the prophet is saying that the time is coming when the people will repent of their conclusions and declarations about the advantages of the godless and the disadvantages of being righteous (cf. Isa. 65:13; Ps. 1; Daniel 12:2; Matt. 25:32ff.). They will repent of the accusations which they had made against God (cf. Job 42:1-6).

DESTRUCTION OF THE WICKED (4:1)

4:1 "For behold, the day is coming, burning like a stove; and all the proud and all who keep on doing unrighteousness will be straw; and the day that is coming will burn them up," says Yahweh of hosts, "so that it will leave to them neither root nor branch."

Some Hebrew manuscripts, the Septuagint, and the Vulgate begin a new chapter with 4:1. English translations have followed this pattern. The Masoretic Hebrew text, however, has continued chapter 3 to the end of the book. When considering the text of 3:13-18, the wisdom of continuing the chapter without a break is logical.

"For behold the day is coming," with the emphasis on "day," is in keeping with other prophetic utterances relative to the day of Yahweh (cf. Obadiah 15-21; Joel 1:15; 2:1-3; 3:14-21; Amos 5:18-20). This is an eschatological emphasis, looking to the consummation of the age. Although it looks to the future, it is kept alive by the interventions of Yahweh in redemption and judgment at various intervals throughout history. It is important that the word "behold" calls attention to something unique and is placed in the text so as to give emphasis to this fact. This is Yahweh's answer to the tirades of the skeptics (cf. 2:17; 3:13-15). It is a further clarification of 3:18.

The day which is coming is the day of Yahweh. It will be the time of the distinction between the righteous and the wicked. The justice of Yahweh, the advantages of the righteous, and the folly of wickedness will be revealed. The primary concern of the prophet is to vindicate Yahweh as a God of righteousness and justice. He also provides comfort for the despondent righteous who were singing a funeral dirge regarding their fortunes and charging God with injustice.

"Burning like a stove" is descriptive of judgment "when all the arrogant and all evil doers will be stubble; the day that comes will burn them up,' says Yahweh of hosts. . . ." Fire, in its association with the holiness of God, often symbolizes cleansing and judgment. It is prominent in prophetic proclamation (cf. Isa. 3:2-3; 10:16-19; Jer. 21:14; Ezek. 20:47-49; Amos 1:3f.; Nahum 1:5-6; Zeph. 1:18, 3:8). The language in Malachi is made graphic by the use of participles. As one reads his words, he can see the flames leaping up and hear the crackling of the fire. It is a time of terror and destruction. The wicked will be destroyed like a handful of grass which is thrown into a bellowing fire. Speaking of the fate of evil doers and the workers of unrighteousness, the psalmist says, "For they will soon fade like the grass, and wither like the green herb" (cf. 37:2).

The arrogant are the self-sufficient ones (see vs. 15 above). "And those who keep on doing unrighteousness" are the associates of the proud in rebellion and sin. The word "unrighteous" may be translated as "wickedness." It denotes the absence of righteousness. Its predominant use in the Old

Testament depicts the character and conduct of those who turn away from God and his way. It describes a cause that is unrighteous (cf. Ex. 23:7). Those who are guilty of sin and liable to punishment are characterized as wicked ones (cf. Gen. 18:23; Num. 35:31). This language is used with reference to wealth that is acquired by wicked and fraudulent balances and other false dealing (cf. Micah 6:10-11; Prov. 8:7).

These arrogant, unrighteous workers of evil are portrayed as worthless chaff. They are marked for total destruction by the terms "root" and "branch" (cf. Isa. 5:24; Nahum 1:10; Obad. 18; Zeph. 2:2; Amos 2:9; Ps. 1:4). The emphasis on complete destruction is not to be taken to mean annihilation. According to the Old Testament concept of judgment, it applies to this life and pertains to that which is physical. The language gives assurance that the wicked will meet with severe and sufficient punishment.

PRESERVATION OF THE GODLY (4:2-3)

4:2 **"But the sun of righteousness shall arise with healing in her wings to you who reverence my name. You shall go forth and leap like calves from the stall.**

3 **And you shall tread down the wicked, because they will be worthless ashes under the soles of your feet in the day which I am going on making," says Yahweh of hosts.**

The basic emphasis is in the vivid contrast in verses 1 and 2. Although the sun is not mentioned in verse 1, it well may be a symbol of the blazing fire that brings destruction to the wicked and the gentle rays quietly overshadowing the righteous. The effect of the sun is determined by that upon which it shines. It hardens clay and melts wax. The gospel has the same effect. It is the means of condemning and hardening unbelievers, while it liberates and softens those who believe (cf. 2 Cor. 2:15-16).

Some have taken the KJV translation, "Sun," with a capital letter, to be a reference to Christ. There are many references in the New Testament to Christ as the righteous one and as our righteousness, but it does not seem that the prophet is referring to him here. There is no person referred to in this text. The whole construction must be considered. The dominant words are "righteousness" and "healing." The "sun of righteousness" is a figure of speech, a symbol of the righteousness of Yahweh. It is the light in the world of morals which dispels the darkness of sin and despair. It gives life and brings strength and healing for sorrow and sickness (cf. Ps. 84:11; 2 Sam. 23:4; Isa. 9:2; Ps. 37:6). The sun image suggests a quiet permeation, impartiality, and universality. Calvin declared that:

> There is nothing, we know, more cheering and healing than rays of the sun; for ill-savour would soon overwhelm us, even within a day, were not the sun to purge the earth from its dregs; and without the sun there would be no respiration. We also feel a sort of relief at the rising of the sun; for the night is a kind of burden. When the sun sets, we feel as it were a heaviness in all our members; and the sick are exhilarated in the morning and experience a change from the influence of the sun; for it brings to us a healing in its wing.[1]

The sun played a vital role in the religions of the ancient Near East. It was worshipped as the god of justice, and it was associated with fertility. Its setting and rising again were associated with the theology of a dying and a rising god. "In its wings" may be associated with the winged solar dials which symbolized the sun's rays as a source of protection and prosperity. Righteousness may suggest vindication, justice, and victory.[2] Malachi uses righteousness instead of salvation to portray a righteous order in which the wicked will be delivered and blessed. The blessing which is provided by the sun of righteousness is designated as being the property of those who fear or reverently worship the name of Yahweh (cf. Gen. 4:26; 12:8; Joel 2:32; Ps. 105:1).

"You shall go forth and leap like calves from the stall." The glory, liberation, and victory which are provided for the

---

[1] John Calvin, *Zechariah and Malachi*, Commentaries on the Twelve Minor Prophets, trans. by John Owen, Vol. V (Grand Rapids: Wm. B. Eerdmans Publishing Company, 1950), p. 620.

[2] J. M. P. Smith, Ward. and Bewer, *A Critical and Exegetical Commentary on the Book of Malachi*, p. 80.

righteous and their knowledge and assurance of the defeat of the wicked provide an occasion for great rejoicing (cf. Isa. 35:10; 55:12; Jer. 33:11; Isa. 12:5-6). It is symbolized by the joy, freedom, and exuberance of young calves which are turned out of their dark stalls and go leaping and springing about into the wide open pastures to enjoy the freedom, warmth, and light of the morning sun. This language of the farm speaks volumes to one who has witnessed what it describes.

As a further symbol of the triumph of the righteous it is declared, "and you shall tread down the wicked, because they shall be as *worthless* ashes under the soles of your feet." The language here is highly figurative and symbolic. Following a strictly literal interpretation, some have used this verse to support their doctrine of the annihilation of the wicked. This would be to reduce man's total being to ashes. It also pictures the triumph of the righteous over the wicked in a way that must be considered as a figure of speech. Dentan observed:

> The imagery of this verse is not attractive to the Christian, but is intended merely to picture as vividly as possible the complete triumph of the good and the defeat of the wicked.[1]

This verse is to be considered in the light of Hebrew eschatology as it is declared in the Old Testament (cf. Micah 4:13; 7:10; Obadiah 18; Isa. 66:24; Zech. 10:5). Malachi sees the punishment of the wicked as the work of the Lord that will come to pass in the day which he is going on making (cf. Deut. 32:35; Rom. 12:19). A thorough study of the New Testament must be made for a more complete understanding of the biblical teaching regarding the judgment, life after death, the rewards of the righteous, and the punishment of the wicked. The Old Testament revelation is not adequate in these things. Its teaching is true, but it is not sufficient.

CONCLUSION: LAW AND PROPHECY TO BE UTILIZED TO BRING THE NATION TO GOD BEFORE HE STRIKES IN JUDGMENT (4:4-6)

4:4 Remember the law of Moses my servant, which I

[1] Dentan, "The Book of Malachi," p. 1143.

> commanded him in Horeb for all Israel, statutes and
> ordinances.
>
> 5 Behold, I am sending to you Elijah the prophet before
> the great and awe-inspiring day of Yahweh comes.
>
> 6 And he will cause to turn the hearts of the fathers to
> their children and the hearts of the children to their
> fathers, lest I proceed to come and I will smite the earth
> with a curse.

Malachi emphasizes the law and covenants throughout his book. They constitute a bridle against sin and a challenge to righteousness. The words, "remember the law of Moses my servant, which I commanded him in Horeb for all Israel, statutes and ordinances," constitute an emphatic call to obedience. All of the terms in this verse are characteristic of Deuteronomy and the Deuteronomic school of thought (cf. Deut. 34:5; Josh. 8:3ff.; 23:6; 1 Kings 2:3; 2 Kings 23:25). The divine origin of the law in its revelation by Yahweh to Moses at Horeb for all Israel emphasizes its authority and demands for all time. In considering the messages of the prophets on the basis of Israel's life, Scott declared:

> Their references to the true native tradition of the Israelite people, and to the period of Moses and the wilderness, exhibit the covenant with Yahweh as a Magna Carta which had brought *this* people into being and conditioned her distinctive historical existence.[1]

That which was proclaimed at Horeb, including the civil and ceremonial regulations known as "statutes and judgments" must be observed (cf. Lev. 26:46; Deut. 4:8). The law is sometimes regarded as the ten commandments, the covenant code and related ordinances, and laws pertaining to the sanctuary and worship (cf. Ex. 20:1-17; 20:22-23:33; 24:1-12; 31:12-18; 34:17-28). The Pentateuch, the first five books of the canon, is sometimes referred to as the law (cf. Josh. 1:7-8; 8:31; 1 Kings 2:3). The entire Old Testament is sometimes regarded as the law (cf. Jno. 12:34; 1 Cor. 14:21). The writer of the book of Ecclesiastes concluded his book by saying, "The end of the matter; all has been heard. Fear God, and keep his command-

---

[1] R. B. Y. Scott, *The Relevance of the Prophets*, pp. 175-76.

ments; for this is the whole duty of man" (cf. 12:13). It is fitting that Malachi should conclude his prophecy and the entire Old Testament with the emphasis which is one of its loudest and clearest notes.

Associated with the law of Moses is Elijah the prophet, perhaps a unique representative of all of the prophets from Enoch to Malachi (see discussion of 3:1a). The law and the prophets had played a vital role in the history of Israel and the kingdom of God and were to continue to do so. Both Moses and Elijah were prominent in Israel's life. The former was present when the nation was born and served as the covenant mediator. The latter stood in the gap and called the people back to reaffirmation and renewal of the covenant in one of the most critical times in the life of the nation. Malachi in a sense calls on his people to bathe their souls in the ancient traditions of the past. It may be considered to be a challenge to ". . . look to the rock from which you were hewn, and to the quarry from which you were digged" (Isa. 51:1). It sounds like a call to covenant renewal as two of their most outstanding covenant personalities look on.

The importance of the law of Moses and the declaration concerning the coming of Elijah the prophet emphasize the compassionate concern of Yahweh for his people who are sure to come to judgment. Thus it is hardly tenable that Malachi is magnifying the place of the law and declaring that the sun has set on prophecy. He is emphasizing the significance of both for his generation and for ours as well. Much of our preaching today must be concerned with the proclamation of the law and the prophets if we are to declare the whole counsel of God.

The law and the prophets were used of God in preparing for the coming of the Messiah. Isaiah and Micah magnified the role of the law as they looked to the latter days when Yahweh would establish his kingdom (cf. Isa. 2:2-4; Micah 4:1-5). The law and the prophets were followed by Jesus in his personal life and in his preaching and teaching (cf. Matt. 5:17ff.). In the parable of the rich man and Lazarus he said, "they have Moses and the prophets; let them hear them" (Luke 16:29). Jesus declared that he came not to destroy the law or the prophets, but to fulfill them (cf. Matt. 5:17-18). At the conclusion of his earthly ministry he spoke solemnly of the fact that he had fulfilled the law and the prophets (cf. Luke 24:44). If the preacher and teacher are to follow in the footsteps of the Master, they have need to live by and proclaim the message of the law and the prophets with all courage, clarity, and compassion.

The prophet Elijah, whose name means "Yahweh is my God," exercised a unique ministry in Israel in the days of Ahab and Jezebel in the ninth century B.C. He was a man of courage, prayer, and unswerving loyalty to Yahweh God. It was either Yahweh or Baal when he called on the nation to make its decision on Mt. Carmel (cf. 1 Kings 17:1ff.).

How is Malachi's declaration of the coming of Elijah the prophet to be understood? Will Elijah return in person as the Jews and some of the early church fathers believed? Will another person come in the spirit and power of Elijah, or will he represent a revival of the order of the prophets? Some have seen Nehemiah, Ezra, or some other leader as an immediate fulfillment of this prophecy. It also has been considered to be expressive of the triumph of God and the forces of righteousness in an evil time like unto that of Elijah. Matthews has observed:

> Such characters, Elijah, Enoch, Moses, are always good subjects for the crystallization of later hopes. Their return from the other world to the scenes of their earthly activity to accomplish by supernatural power the thing that was humanly impossible was a rather prevalent conception. Even in the profane world we find a similar idea in a Cyrus, a Caesar, a Nero, and a Napoleon redivivus, while in Judaism many of the ancestors were believed to return occasionally for the sake of their suffering posterity (Matt. 11:3, 14; 14:2).[1]

It is significant that Elijah did appear with Moses on the mount of transfiguration and the two of them talked with Jesus regarding his decease (cf. Matt. 17:1-8). It may be surmised that they declared that the law and the prophets could not provide salvation and encouraged Jesus to go on to the cross. It was after this unique experience that the disciples raised the question with Jesus about the coming of Elijah which was said to be a teaching of the scribes (cf. Matt. 17:10). The reply of

[1]Matthews, "Malachi," p. 35.

Jesus, stating that Elijah had already come, was taken by the disciples to mean that he was speaking to them about John the Baptist (cf. Matt. 17:9-13). This language has a note of finality about it.

Malachi's emphasis on the coming of Elijah the prophet in conjunction with his pronouncements on the law of Moses is a fitting conclusion to his work. Both the law and the prophets are effectively utilized throughout the Book of Malachi. They emphasize the fact of sin, the necessity of repentance in the conversion of sinners, and the ushering in of the Day of Yahweh. It is the use of effective forces which were provided by the Lord as a means of turning the nation to Yahweh before the judgment falls. It must be remembered that the offices of the law and the prophets were fulfilled in Christ, and their messages are magnified wherever the teachings of Jesus are proclaimed.

If the declaration regarding the coming of Elijah looked to the actual return of this prophet to the earth at any time, it is safe to say that Jesus would have declared it instead of pointing to John the Baptist as the fulfillment of the spirit of this prophecy. The times in which John the Baptist exercised his ministry had striking parallels to the day of Elijah. One was to come who would stand in the spirit, courage, and power of Elijah to arrest a godless people and cause them to seek God in repentance and faith. It may be that the emphasis on Elijah indicates the need for a neo-Elijah type of spirit and preaching to deal with the prevailing moral and spiritual problems.

New Testament references reveal that John the Baptist was the fulfillment of Isaiah 40:3, Malachi 3:1, and 4:5 (cf. Matt. 3:1-12; Mark 1:2-8; Luke 3:2-18; 7:27; Matt. 11:10; 17:11; Mark 9:11). John 1:21 is a denial that John was Elijah, but it is not a denial that he was one who had come in the spirit and power of Elijah.

Several of the prophets looked for a new David, a David redivivus who would reign over a new Israel, redeemed and cleansed (cf. Isa. 9:1-7; 11:1-5; Mic. 5:2-4; Hos. 3:5; Jer. 30:9; Ezek. 34:23f.; 37:24f.). We are not to think of a resurrection and return of David, Israel's ideal king, who had been dead for centuries, but of a shepherd king who was to be in his reign the unique one, standing above all others as David did. These prophecies had their fulfillment in Christ. Interpreters who declare that there will be a literal return of Elijah before the second coming of Christ do not see a literal return of David before Christ comes again.

A belief that the prophecy of Malachi concerning the coming of Elijah will be fulfilled in advance of the second coming of Christ has no support in the Scriptures and would not serve any useful purpose when Jesus does return. The prophets of the Old Testament were not concerned with the second coming of Christ. Their concern was that he would come the first time (cf. Isa. 9:6-7; 11:1-5; Micah 5:2-5; Mal. 3:1-3). The second coming of Christ is a New Testament doctrine. If there were things which the prophets envisioned that the Messiah would do that have not taken place, their accomplishment since his coming or when he comes again was not their concern. They planned no program nor did they set a time schedule for the Messiah and his work.

The work which the Elijah-like prophet is to accomplish is described in the first part of verse 5. A cursory examination of the passage suggests that he will build a bridge across the generation gap and promote love and unity between parents and children. Such an emphasis may be a partial concern of the prophet because there were estrangements and serious difficulties in family life that needed to be faced and overcome. This could have been a reversion to the divorce and heathen marriage problem that produced serious divisions in domestic life and promoted the worship of pagan gods. This worship, among other things, could have been that of a Babylonian, a Persian, or a Greek cult with certain corrupting and degrading philosophies which threatened to destroy all home life.

It may be that Malachi regards the children as the people of his day who had become corrupt and were not walking after the teachings of the law and the prophets as did the more godly ancestors of the nation. He envisions a time to come when the way of the fathers will become the way of the children. This will produce an obedient, covenant keeping community that will do justly, love mercy (covenant love), and walk humbly with God (cf. Mic. 6:6-8).

The Hebrew word *cherem* is translated "curse," "ban," "devote," or "exterminate." It is sometimes used in the setting apart of certain people or things for sacred use or to mark them for destruction. Its use by Malachi is to pronounce the curse of destruction to be visited upon hardened, impenitent sinners. The concern in magnifying the law of Moses and the coming of Elijah the prophet is to emphasize the longsuffering and lovingkindness of God in seeking to bring the nation to repentance as a means of avoiding the ban (cf. Ex. 22:20; Lev. 27:28-29; Josh. 6:17; 1 Sam. 15:3; 1 Kings 20:42; Isa. 34:5). Thus Malachi, like Isaiah, Lamentations, and Ecclesiastes, ends with a word of desolation, a curse. The Jews follow a practice of repeating the next to the last verse of the last three of these books in order to end the reading on a brighter and more victorious note. In the case of Malachi, verse 4 of the last chapter is repeated by the Jews after verse 6, thereby concluding the prophecy with a command that gives prominence to the law of Moses. It should be stated here that there is not a bright note for sinners who meet God in their impenitence. An effort to soften the terms and sweeten the language will not do away with the judgment to be visited by the Almighty.

The final verses of Malachi, a fitting conclusion to the book, add the last stroke of the brush to the magnificent portrait of the Old Testament prophets.

It is the prayer of this writer that he and his readers may continue to experience the divine love which is proclaimed by the one who is designated as "my messenger." For his message is like the last rays of the setting sun which brings the era of the Old Covenant of divine love to a close, and awaits the bright radiance of the rising of the sun of the New Covenant of divine love revealed in the person and work of Jesus Christ.

Selected Bibliography

Ackroyd, Peter. *Exile and Restoration.* Philadelphia: The Westminster Press, 1968.

Anderson, Bernhard W. *Understanding the Old Testament.* 2nd ed. Englewood Cliffs, N. J.: Prentice-Hall, Incorporated, 1957.

Anderson, G. W. *A Critical Introduction to the Old Testament.* London: Duchworth, 1959.

Baab, Otto. *Prophetic Preaching: A New Approach.* Nashville: Abingdon Press, 1958.

———. *The Theology of the Old Testament.* Nashville: Abingdon-Cokesbury, 1959.

Beecher, Willis J. *The Prophets and the Promise. Reprint.* Grand Rapids: Baker Book House, 1963.

Bennett, T. Miles. "Malachi." *The Broadman Bible Commentary*. Vol VII. Nashville: Broadman Press, 1972.

Bentzen, Aage. *Introduction to the Old Testament.* Copenhagen: G. E. C. Gads Forlag, 1948.

Bewer, Julius A. *The Book of the Twelve Prophets.* Vol. II. New York: Harper & Brothers, 1949.

Bishop, Eric F. F. *Prophets of Palestine.* London: Lutterworth Press, 1962.

Blackwood, Andrew Watterson. *Preaching from the Prophetic Books.* Nashville: Abingdon-Cokesbury Press, 1951.

Bright, John. *A History of Israel.* Philadelphia: Westminister Press, 1974.

_____. The *Kingdom of God.* Nashville: Abingdon-Cokesbury Press, 1953.

Brown, Francis; Driver, S. R.; and Briggs, Charles A. *A Hebrew and English Lexicon of the Old Testament.* Boston and New York: Houghton Mifflin Company, 1907.

Buber, Martin. *The Prophetic Faith.* Translated by Carlyle Witton-Davies. New York: Harper, 1960.

Calkins, Raymond A. *The Modern Message of the Minor Prophets.* New York: Harper & Brothers, 1947.

Calvin, John. *Zechariah and Malachi.* Commentaries on the Twelve Minor Prophets. Translated by John Owen. Vol. V. Grand Rapids: Wm. B. Eerdmans Publishing Company, 1950.

Cartledge, Samuel A. *A Conservative Introduction to the Old Testament.* Grand Rapids, Mich.: Zondervan Publishing House, 1943.

Cashdan, Eli. "Malachi." *The Twelve Prophets.* Edited by A. Cohen. Bournemouth: The Soncino Press, 1948.

Cohon, B. D. *The Prophets: Their Personalities and Teachings.* New York: Bloch Publishing Co., 1960.

Cripps, Robert S. *A Critical and Exegetical Commentary on the Book of Amos.* Reprint ed. London: S. P. C. K., 1969.

Davidson, A. B. *Hebrew Syntax*. 3rd ed. Edinburgh: T. & T. Clark, 1964.

______. *Old Testament Prophecy*. Edited by J. A. Paterson. Edinburgh: T. & T. Clark, 1903.

______. *The Theology of the Old Testament*. Edited by S. D. F. Salmond. Edinburgh: T. & T. Clark, 1904.

Davidson, John. "Malachi." *Temple Dictionary of the Bible*. 1910.

Davis, John D. *A Dictionary of the Bible*. 4th revised ed. Philadelphia: Westminister Press, 1924.

______, ed. *The Westminister Dictionary of the Bible*. 5th ed. revised and rewritten by Henry S. Gehman. Philadelphia: Westminister Press, 1944.

Deere, Derward W. *The Twelve Speak*. Vol II. New York: The American Press, 1961.

Dentan, Robert C. "The Book of Malachi." *The Interpreter's Bible*. Edited by George Arthur Buttrick. Vol. VI. New York: Abingdon Press, 1956.

Driver, S. R. *An Introduction to the Literature of the Old Testament*. New York: Charles Scribner's Sons, 1906.

______. *The Ideals of the Prophets*. Edinburgh: T. & T. Clark, 1915.

______, ed. *The Minor Prophets Nahum, Habakkuk, Zephaniah, Haggai, Zechariah, Malachi*. The Century Bible. Edited by Walter F. Adeney. New York: Henry Frowde, 1906.

Dummelow, J. R., ed. *A Commentary on the Holy Bible*. New York: Macmillan Company, 1936.

Eichrodt, Walther. *Theology of the Old Testament*. 2 vols. Translated by John Baker. Philadelphia: Westminister Press, 1967.

Eiselen, F. C. *The Minor Prophets*. New York: Eaton and Mains, 1907.

Eissfeldt, Otto. *The Old Testament: An Introduction*. Translated by Peter R. Ackroyd. New York: Harper & Row, 1965.

Elmslie, W. A. L. *How Came Our Faith*. Cambridge: University Press, 1948.

Farrar, F. W. *The Minor Prophets*. New York: Fleming H. Revell Company, n.d.

Fohrer, Georg. *Introduction to the Old Testament*. Translated by David E. Green. Nashville: Abingdon Press, 1968.

Fowler, Henry T. *The Prophets as Statesmen and Preachers*. Boston: Pilgrim Press, 1904.

Francisco, Clyde T. *Introducing the Old Testament*. Nashville: Broadman Press, 1950.

Gailey, James H., Jr., ed. *Micah, Habakkuk, Nahum, Zephaniah, Haggai, Zechariah, Malachi*. The Layman's Bible Commentary. Edited by Balmer H. Kelly. Vol. XV. Richmond: John Knox Press, 1967.

Gesenius, William. *Hebrew and Chaldee Lexicon*. Translated by Samuel Prideaux Tregelles. Grand Rapids: Wm. B. Eerdmans Publishing Company, 1969.

Girdlestone, Robert Baker. *Synonyms of the Old Testament*. Grand Rapids: Wm. B. Eerdmans Publishing Co., 1948.

Gordon, Alex R. *The Prophets of the Old Testament*. 2nd ed. London: Hodder and Stoughton, 1919.

Gordon, Cyrus H. *The World of the Old Testament*. 2nd ed. Garden City, N. Y.: Doubleday & Company, Inc., 1958.

Gottwald, Norman K. *A Light to the Nations*. New York: Harper and Brothers, 1959.

Gray, George Buchanan. *A Critical Introduction to the Old Testament*. New York: Charles Scribner's Sons, 1913.

Hailey, Homer. *A Commentary on the Minor Prophets*. Grand Rapids: Baker Book House, 1972.

Harper, William R. *Elements of Hebrew Syntax by an Inductive Method*. 2nd ed. Chicago: The Hebrew Book Exchange, 1882.

Harrington, Wilfrid J. *The Record of the Promise*. Chicago: Priory Press, 1965.

Harrison, R. K. *Introduction to the Old Testament.* Grand Rapids, Mich.: William B. Eerdmans Publishing Company, 1969.

Herbert, A. S. *Worship in Ancient Israel.* Ecumenical Studies in Worship. Richmond: John Knox Press, 1965.

Heschel, Abraham J. *The Prophets.* New York: Harper and Row, 1962.

Holliday, William L. *A Concise Hebrew and Aramaic Lexicon of the Old Testament.* Based upon the lexical work of Ludwig Koehler and Walter Baumgartner. Grand Rapids: William B. Eerdmans, 1971.

Jacob, Edmond. *Theology of the Old Testament.* Translated by Arthur W. Heathcote and Philip J. Allcock. New York: Harper & Brothers Publishers, 1958.

Jacobus, Melancthon W.; Nourse, Edward E.; and Zenos, Andrew C., editors. *A New Standard Bible Dictionary.* Funk & Wagnalls Company, 1926.

Jones, D. R. *Haggai, Zechariah and Malachi.* Torch Bible Commentaries. London: SCM Press, 1962.

Jordan, W. G. *Prophetic Ideas and Ideals.* New York: Fleming H. Revell Company, 1902.

Keil, Carl F. and Delitzsch, F. *The Twelve Minor Prophets.* Biblical Commentary on the Old Testament. Vol. II. Grand Rapids: Wm. B. Eerdmans Publishing Co., 1949.

Kelly, William. *Lectures Introductory to the Study of the Minor Prophets.* London: W. H. Broom, 1874.

Kennedy, J. Hardee. "Joel." *The Broadman Bible Commentary.* Edited by Clifton J. Allen. Vol. VII. Nashville: Broadman Press, 1972.

Kittel, Rudolf, ed. *Biblia Hebraica.* 7th ed. Stuttgart: Privilegierte Wurttembergische Bibelanstalt, 1951.

Kraeling, E. G. "Malachi." *Dictionary of the Bible.* 2nd revised ed.

Kirkpatrick, A. F. *The Doctrine of the Prophets.* 3rd ed. London: Macmillan and Co., Limited, 1906.

Knudson, Albert C. *The Beacon Lights of Prophecy.* New York: Eaton and Mains, 1914.

_____. *The Prophetic Movement in Israel.* New York: Abdingdon-Cokesbury Press, 1921.

Kuhl, Curt. *The Prophets of Israel.* Richmond, Va.: John Knox Press, 1960.

Laetsch, Theo. *Bible Commentary: The Minor Prophets.* St. Louis, Mo.: Concordia Publishing House, 1956.

Lindblom, J. *Prophecy in Ancient Israel.* Philadelphia: Fortress Press, 1962.

McFadyen, John Edgar. *Introduction to the Old Testament.* New York: A. C. Armstrong and Son, 1905.

_____. *Old Testament Scenes and Characters.* London: James Clarke and Co., Limited, 1928.

McKenzie, John L. *Dictionary of the Bible.* London-Dublin: Geoffrey Chapman, 1965.

Maclaren, Alexander. *The Books of Ezekiel, Daniel, and the Minor Prophets.* Expositions of Holy Scripture. Vol. VI. Grand Rapids: Wm. B. Eerdmans Publishing Co., 1959.

Matthews, I. G. "Haggai, Malachi." *An American Commentary on the Old Testament.* Philadelphia: The American Baptist Publication Society, 1935.

Mays, James Luther. *Hosea A Commentary.* The Old Testament Library. Edited by G. Ernest Wright, John Bright, James Barr, and Peter Ackroyd. Philadelphia: Westminster Press, 1969.

Miller, Medeleine S. and Miller, J. Lane. *Harper's Bible Dictionary.* 3rd ed. New York: Harper & Brothers, Publishers, 1952.

Mitchell, Hinckley G.; Smith, J. M. Powis; and Bewer, Julius A. *A Critical and Exegetical Commentary on Haggai, Zechariah, Malachi, and Jonah.* The International Critical Commentary. Edinburgh: T. & T. Clark, 1912.

Moore, T. V. *The Prophets of the Restoration.* New York: Robert Carter and Brothers, 1856.

_____. *Haggai and Malachi*. Reprint. New York: Robert Carter, 1960.

Morgan, G. Campbell. *The Voices of Twelve Hebrew Prophets*. New York: Fleming H. Revell Company, n.d.

Napier, B. Davie. *From Faith to Faith*. New York: Harper & Brothers, Publishers, 1955.

_____. *Song of the Vineyard*. New York: Harper and Brothers, 1962.

Neil, W. "Malachi." *The Interpreter's Dictionary of the Bible*. Vol. III. 1962.

Noth, Martin. *The History of Israel*. Revised ed. London: Adam and Charles Black, 1960.

Paterson, John. *The Goodly Fellowship of the Prophets*. New York: Charles Scribner's Sons, 1948.

Perowne, T. T. *Malachi, with Notes and Introduction*. The Cambridge Bible for Schools and Colleges. Cambridge: University Press, 1896.

Pfeiffer, Charles F. *Exile and Return*. Grand Rapids, Mich.: Baker Book House, 1962.

Pfeiffer, Robert H. *Introduction to the Old Testament*. New York: Harper and Brothers, 1948.

_____. *The Books of the Old Testament*. New York: Harper & Brothers Publishers, 1957.

Pusey, E. B. *The Minor Prophets, A Commentary*. Vol. II. Grand Rapids: Baker Book House, 1950.

Rad, Gerhard von. *Old Testament Theology*, II. Translated by D. M. G. Stalker. New York: Harper and Row, 1965.

_____. *The Message of the Prophets*. London: SCM Press, 1968.

Robinson, George L. "Malachi." *The International Standard Bible Encyclopaedia*. 1915. Vol. III.

_____. *The Twelve Minor Prophets*. New York: George H. Doran Company, 1926.

Robinson, H. Wheeler. *The Religious Ideas of the Old Testament*. Great Britain: Edinburgh University Press, 1938.

Robinson, Theodore H. *An Introduction of the Old Testament*. Reprint. London: Edward Arnold & Company, 1952.

______. *Prophecy and the Prophets in Ancient Israel*. London: Duckworth, 1923.

Rowley, H. H. *The Biblical Doctrine of Election*. London: Lutterworth Press, 1964.

______. *The Faith of Israel*. London: SCM Press, Limited, 1956.

Scott, R. B. Y. *The Relevance of the Prophets*. New York: The Macmillian Company, 1957.

Sellin, E. *Introduction to the Old Testament*. Translated by W. Montgomery. London: Hodder and Stoughton, Limited, 1923.

Smith, George Adam. *Jeremiah*. 4th ed. New York: Harper and Brothers Publishers, 1929.

______. *The Book of the Twelve Prophets*. Vol. II. New and revised edition. London: Hodder and Stoughton, 1928.

Smith, J. M. P.; Ward, W. H.; and Bewer, Julius A. *A Critical and Exegetical Commentary on the Book of Malachi*. The International Critical Commentary. Edited by Samuel Rolles Driver, Alfred Plummer, and Charles Augustus. Edinburgh: T. & T. Clark, 1912.

Smith, W. R. and Torrey, C. C. "Malachi." *Encyclopaedia Biblica*. 1902. Vol. III.

Snaith, Norman H. *The Distinctive Ideas of the Old Testament*. London: The Epworth Press, 1944.

Snaith, Norman H. *The Jews from Cyrus to Herod*. Wallington, Surrey: The Religious Education Press, LTD, 1949.

Stack, Richard and Torshell, Samuel. *A Commentary Upon the Prophecy of Malachi*. Edinburgh: James Nichol, 1865.

Stagg, Frank. *New Testament Theology*. Nashville: Broadman Press, 1962.

Steinmueller, John E. and Kathryn Sullivan. *Catholic Biblical Encyclopedia Old Testament*. New York: Joseph F. Wagner, Inc. Publishers, 1956.

Storer, J. W. *The Major Messages of the Minor Prophets*. Nashville: Broadman Press, 1940.

The Holy Bible: Revised Standard Version. New York: Thomas Nelson and Sons, 1952.

Taylor, Barnard C. *Prophecy and the Prophets*. Philadelphia: The Judson Press, 1923.

Unger, Merrill F. *Guide to the Old Testament*. Grand Rapids: Zondervan, 1956.

Vriezen, Th. C. *An Outline of Old Testament Theology*. English ed. Newton, Mass.: 1958.

Watts, John D. W. *Obadiah: A Critical Exegetical Commentary*. Grand Rapids: Wm. B. Eerdmans Publishing Co., 1969.

______. "Zechariah." *The Broadman Bible Commentary*.

Watts, J. Wash. *A Distinctive Translation of Genesis*. Grand Rapids: Wm. B. Eerdmans Publishing Co., 1963.

______. *A Survey of Syntax in the Hebrew Old Testament*. Grand Rapids: Wm. B. Eerdmans Publishing Co., 1964.

______. *Old Testament Teaching*. Nashville: Broadman Press, 1967.

Weingreen, J. *A Practical Grammar for Classical Hebrew*. 2nd ed. Oxford: Clarendon Press, 1959.

Weiser, Arthur. *Introduction to the Old Testament*. Translated by Dorothea M. Barton. London: Darton, Longman and Todd, Ltd., 1961.

______. *The Old Testament: Its Formation and Development*. New York: Association Press, 1961.

Welch, A. C. "Malachi." *Dictionary of the Bible*. 1900. Vol. III.

Williams, Ronald J. *Hebrew Syntax: An Outline.* Toronto: University of Toronto Press, 1967.

Williams, Walter G. *The Prophets: Pioneers to Christianity.* New York: Abingdon Press, 1956.

Yates, Kyle M. *Preaching from the Prophets.* New York: Harper and Brothers Publishers, 1942.

Yoder, S. C. *He Gave Some Prophets.* Scottdale, Pa.: Herald Press, 1964.

Young, Edward J. *An Introduction to the Old Testament.* Grand Rapids: Wm. B. Eerdmans Publishing Co., 1949.

______. *My Servants the Prophets.* Grand Rapids: Wm. B. Eerdmans, 1952.

Young, Robert. *Analytical Concordance to the Bible.* Revised by Wm. B. Stevenson. New York: Funk and Wagnalls Co., n.d.